PATHFINDER BENNETT— AIRMAN EXTRAORDINARY

PATHFINDER BENNETT—
AIRMAN EXTRAORDINARY

AIR VICE MARSHAL D. C. T. BENNETT
CB CBE DSO

A. S. Jackson

TERENCE DALTON LIMITED
LAVENHAM, SUFFOLK 1991

Published by
TERENCE DALTON LIMITED
ISBN 0 86138 088 6
© A. S. Jackson 1991

Text photoset in 10/11 pt. Baskerville
Printed in Great Britain at
The Lavenham Press Limited, Lavenham, Suffolk

Contents

For
Anderley

Acknowledgements

I AM most grateful to Mrs Ly Bennett for the loan of many photographs. Others were made available by the Royal Air Force Museum, the Royal Australian Air Force Museum, the Canadian Forces Photo Unit, *Master* magazine, Captain R. Alabaster, Captain K. Hagyard, Mr V. Bingham, Mr C. Cheesman, Mr M. Carr, and Mr D. Munro. Essential information was provided by the Air Historical Branch of the Ministry of Defence, Air Marshal Sir Ivor Broom, who kindly wrote the foreword, Mr R. Wilson, archivist of British Airways, Mr M. Tagg, custodian of the Woods Humphery Collection, Captain D. Walbourn, Mr K. Hayward, and Mr H. Pusey.

Finally I wish to thank others whose interest and assistance have contributed to my book.

Foreword

THIS BOOK will not only have enormous appeal to all those who knew Don Bennett but will also enthrall the younger generation, who may be unaware of the great contribution he made throughout his life to the development of both civil and military aviation.

The chapter headings in this book are probably enough in themselves to whet the appetite of every aviation enthusiast. The reader is taken through various phases of Don Bennett's life in chronological order. The description of the way in which he organised the ferrying of aircraft (non pressurised of course) in the winter of 1940 from North America to the British Isles is a classic and should be required reading for the present generation of pilots who may perhaps not always appreciate the skills, initiative, determination and sheer airmanship which were necessary to survive in hazardous winter flying conditions some fifty years ago. Experienced navigators were non-existent, the sextant was the basic navigation aid, and, once the ferry route was established, navigators who had just completed their training in Canada joined their first squadron on the journey back to England. They performed wonders. VIPs, who today enjoy the luxury of first class travel had to be content with mattresses in the bomb bay.

We read of Don Bennett's time as a Halifax squadron commander, of the attack he led on the Tirpitz, of the way he evaded capture after crashing in Norway and of his escape back to England via Sweden; the energy, imagination and professionalism he showed in creating the Pathfinder Force, which reduced dramatically the bombing errors of the less experienced crews in the Second World War; the pioneering flights made by British South American Airways to South America in the early post-war years, often with very inadequate navigation aids; the way in which air transport won its spurs on the Berlin airlift—all show facets of the character of this remarkable man.

In each phase of life Don Bennett accomplished more than most people do in a lifetime. The author, himself a very experienced pilot, knew Don Bennett for some forty years and is thus able to highlight from his personal contact the characteristics which kept Don Bennett ever seeking improvements in flying procedures and techniques. Success in one venture was just a springboard for success in the next.

Whenever aviators speak about pioneers of aviation the name of Don Bennett will inevitably soon come into the conversation.

Pioneers like Don Bennett who fought the elements with inadequate equipment have contributed to making flying in a commercial airline safer today than crossing the road in one's home town.

Air Marshal Sir Ivor Broom, KCB, CBE, DSO, DFC, AFC

An Australian in the RAF   1

IT WAS an unwelcome surprise to the parents of Don Bennett
when he announced his intention to join the Royal Australian
Air Force and train to be a pilot. They opposed it on the grounds of
danger and because they rated the pilot's job as little more than
that of an aerial bus driver. Their sons had been educated for
better things: the eldest was already a barrister, their second son
was a doctor and the third was studying for the bar. They had
entertained hopes that their youngest son Don would become the
second doctor in the family.

He was born in 1910 in Toowoomba, Queensland, in the
family home on their cattle station on the rich earth of the Darling
Downs. The greatest influence in his life was his mother, English-
born, who had been taken to Australia as a child and brought up as
a strict Methodist and teetotaller. Don's grandfather was a doctor
who had been in dispute with the British Medical Association. He
used to say that "the only crime an Englishman cannot forgive is to
be right". There were to be many occasions in the future when Don
Bennett would be reminded of this axiom. Among the earliest
hymns which he learnt at his mother's knee was "Dare to be a
Daniel." Certainly he was to live up to that principle.

Perhaps the example of his older brothers, whose education
was marked with distinction, gave the youngest Bennett an initial
sense of failure. More likely he knew he had the brains to learn
enough in time for the examinations. Either way, his school reports
in his final year indicated idleness and his father saw no
justification in meeting the expense of a university course for a
further five years. In addition to the cattle station he managed an
agency business in Brisbane; his son could make himself useful
there. The latter, however, expressed a preference for work on the
cattle station; he wanted time to decide what to do with his life.
Bennett Senior was delighted, envisaging the day in the future
when he could hand over the management of the station to a
younger member of the family.

Don spent three months as a jackaroo performing the
ordinary everyday work of a cattle station hand. He rode the
boundaries armed with an axe, a good pair of pliers and coils of
barbed wire; he mustered cattle, joined in the branding, earmark-
ing and droving tasks. He learnt to make a stock whip and a green

Opposite: *Flying
Officer Bennett, 1935.*
Bennett family

1

hide rope. Every two weeks a steer would be killed for home consumption and they would enjoy the luxury of fresh meat for a day or two before most of the carcase was salted and stored in a strong brine bath until the next killing.

Those three months were long enough for him to realise that his original intention to become a doctor had been in imitation of his grandfather's career and the example of his brothers. It was also a sufficient time to decide that the life of a cattle hand or even a station manager might be happy but it was also a dead end, so he felt no particular regret at abandoning this ambition. The prospects of a business career appealed to him even less, and it was at this point that he made up his mind to embark upon a career in aviation. He left the cattle station and returned to Brisbane to break the news to his parents. Unable to change their son's mind, they prevailed upon his brother, the doctor, to try his powers of dissuasion, as he had flown with the Australian commercial pilots before the flying doctor scheme was established. Dutifully, he stressed the dangers of thunderstorms and mechanical failures, but for Bennett himself "there was only one thing in his letter that mattered and it confirmed my ambition completely. He used the phrase 'better be not at all than not be noble.' He admitted that to forsake one's ambition at the dictate of fear would indeed be ignoble."

Until that time Bennett had had very little to do with aviation beyond helping a neighbour rebuild an old Farman biplane and overhaul its engine, but he always claimed to remember the Wright brothers giving a flying display at Toowoomba before he had even reached his fourth birthday. Later he had seen Bert Hinkler, an Australian pilot during the First World War, arrive on a solo flight from England. He was present later when Amy Johnson, also on a solo flight from the British Isles, overshot the flat meadow of a farm and ran into a cornfield, where her aircraft pitched over. He had also witnessed the arrival of Kingsford Smith at the end of his pioneering flight across the Pacific.

Bennett applied to join the Royal Australian Air Force and thereafter persisted in pursuing his ambition in the face of a number of hurdles. There were several thousand applicants for fifteen vacancies as pilot trainees, but his academic aptitude in physics and science subjects, together with voluntary service in the Australian Citizen Forces, carried weight and he was accepted. The medical board reported him absolutely fit with the exception of his tonsils. Utterly determined to deny the RAAF any opportunity to reject him, he had the offending tonsils removed the same day and reported the operation to the authorities in Melbourne. It cost him a delay of six months and he spent this time in his father's office while he read all the books on flying that he could find and learnt all he could about aircraft.

RAAF cadets at Point Cook, Victoria, Australia, 1930. Bennett is seated to the left of the officer. RAAF

At the end of the six months, eagerly awaiting the day when he could begin his training, Bennett received a letter informing him that as he had been found unfit he would have to re-apply in a year's time. Absolutely determined to avoid further delay, he travelled by train to Sydney, continued on to Melbourne and went straight from the railway station to the Air Board. Surprised but impressed by the young man's resolution, the Board agreed to give him another medical immediately and thereafter assured him that he would most certainly begin the course in six months' time.

Bennett had lived all his life in a hot climate but it was a cold midwinter day in 1930 when he reported to Victoria barracks in Melbourne. After the usual formalities, the fifteen would-be pilots were made aware of an unexpected development. The economic depression which had engulfed Australia and most parts of the world had obliged the government and thus the RAAF to practise economies. Unless the majority of the fifteen new recruits were willing to continue their service in the Royal Air Force in England

3

at the end of their training, they would not be allowed to begin the course. Bennett had never had any urge to travel and certainly no desire to leave Australia for any considerable period, but it required only a few moments' thought before he and most of the others agreed to this condition. Thereupon the young men were ordered to load their possessions on to a service truck which took them to Point Cook on the western shore of Port Philip.

Point Cook was able to accommodate both landplanes and marine aircraft. Two Southampton flying boats and five single-engined Seagull amphibians were provided with a pier and slipway. The hangars and workshops were on the side of the aerodrome nearest the sea, while the living quarters were at the other extremity. "A healthy arrangement for unwanted exercise", Bennett surmised, "but enormously wasteful in man-hours, to the delight no doubt of all regular officers. I was to learn there and at all future stations that the Air Force has no thought whatsoever for economy in manpower in matters such as station geography." Along with some of the other cadets he learnt the first unwritten law of the Air Force, "Thou shalt not be caught", when, ignorant of the regulations, they walked straight across the aerodrome towards the hangars. Their offence became apparent to them when they observed the demeanour of the duty officer as he awaited their arrival. Several cadets turned tail and rapidly retraced their steps; Bennett and the others accepted their fate and were found some uncongenial tasks to perform.

Point Cook in 1930, the initial RAAF training station. RAAF Museum

A week of polishing the floors and their own equipment, drill and physical training was followed by flying practice and practical ground instruction. The day began and ended with the mile-long march to and from the hangars. Two officers and two sergeants gave flying instruction. Bennett was allotted to a Sergeant Preston whom he described as "a solid average type, by no means a genius, but with a simple direct approach to the job of teaching flying which suited me admirably. He made no pretence at heavy theory but taught the practical job extremely well". The cadets were also fortunate to be trained on de Havilland Moths, one of the greatest trainers ever built. Shortly before their arrival a spate of fatal accidents had led to the abandonment of the previous obsolete aircraft, which had their origins in the First World War.

After about eight hours of dual flying instruction, Bennett made his first solo flight. Both solo and dual flying training followed as the cadets were taught how to make stall turns and slow rolls, to loop and thereby to gain confidence in their ability to master their aircraft. A regular feature of their dual instruction was to practise forced landings, essential to the pilot of a single-engined machine. On solo flights the more adventurous cadets enjoyed the excitement of flying low over the countryside, then as now a practice frowned upon by the authorities.

More advanced flying instruction was undertaken on a large single-engined biplane, the Westland Wapiti. As well as piloting the machine, the cadets were introduced to front gunnery at ground targets and rear seat gunnery with Lewis guns at targets in the bay. The cadets carried out camera gun work on each other and flew photographic runs to make mosaics of the area overflown, which they developed, printed and pieced together themselves. Bombing practice was also performed in the Wapiti.

The year's training ended with both flying tests and written examinations. Bennett came top of the class in flying and second in the examinations. He went home to enjoy his embarkation leave before sailing to England, full of pride at the thought that he could claim to be a qualified pilot. The profound economic slump did not tempt the Australian authorities to abandon the custom that serving officers travelled first class and the newly commissioned pilot-officers set sail in the P and O steamship *Narkunda*. After a call at Colombo the ship put into Bombay, where a number of English officers of the Indian Army together with their wives came aboard to begin their home leave. It was Bennett's first experience of the English "en masse". He had expected British Officers to resemble the graduates of the Australian Military College, whose manner and bearing he did not like, but he decided that "the men were not too bad. Of the wives however I can say little good. Mostly they were loud-mouthed, overbearing, pompous and stupid, and I must say I felt that if English ladies were like these examples, then every Englishman must indeed be an unhappy creature. Later on I was to learn better".

His first taste of RAF life was at Uxbridge, then the HQ of Fighting Area. In 1931 the RAF was very small and the period until 1935 when Bennett was serving has been called the "locust years". The locusts were the British people who refused to take seriously the signs of renewed German militancy. The electorate and the political parties were both to blame; less than twenty million pounds was spent each year on the RAF and each year the Labour party ritually opposed even that. The National Government preferred to revive the economy rather than to provide the nation with adequate defences and the quality of the fighting equipment had been deteriorating since 1918. Most of the aircraft still looked very familiar indeed to the veterans of the First World War, the science of navigation had not been developed and the means to navigate were rudimentary in the extreme. Fighters were slow, guns were of wartime design and nothing existed to detect the approach of a hostile low-flying aircraft.

There was only one officers' mess at Uxbridge and Bennett was over-awed by the numbers of very senior officers who took their places at dinner each evening, when mess dress was always worn. Although permitted to continue to wear the RAAF dark blue, the Australians were also required to buy themselves RAF uniforms and were sent off to an approved London tailor. Then they were sent to the Flying Training School near Liverpool where they received a short period of instruction on the Armstrong Whitworth Siskin before being posted to a squadron. It was the first all-metal aircraft to be delivered to the Royal Air Force.

The Siskin was a biplane which Bennett considered to be "undoubtedly one of the worst aeroplanes ever produced . . . not stable in any plane and generally carried a directional bias as well as a one wing down tendency". Even so, for all its faults he was glad to fly this machine and to be able to call himself a "fighter boy", a description which attracted an aura of glamour. Alone among the Australians he was posted to 29 Squadron at North Weald but was delighted to find a graduate from an earlier Point Cook course already there, who was able to give him useful advice. The widespread distrust of the Siskin was reflected by the commander of the squadron, who flew it as seldom as possible himself, banned aerobatics in formation and exercised considerable restraint over all his pilots' activities in the air.

When the squadron commander received orders to introduce night flying practice he was obviously very shaken. The Siskin was a single seat aircraft so no dual practice could be undertaken. To the amusement of Bennett and the other pilots he had the flarepath laid in broad daylight and practised his own landings at dusk. Before darkness fell he taxied in and declared that he would be informing Fighting Area that the Siskin was unsafe for night flying. "Fortunately for us," Bennett observed, "his powerful argument was not accepted and we continued with our night training. Not only was this most valuable flying experience . . . it also taught me a new technique: map-reading by night."

In 1931 radio telephony was in its infancy and he found that the equipment on the Siskin was reminiscent of the early crystal sets of his childhood. Audibility over a range of ten miles was held to be satisfactory and on one historic occasion Bennett achieved two-way communication over forty-three miles. The emphasis on disarmament, peace conferences and economy meant that the fighter squadrons were forbidden to fly with live ammunition. Every summer, however, the squadron moved to Sutton Bridge for two weeks of air-to-ground firing practice at targets on the shores of the Wash. Bennett found it an exhilarating and warlike experience to dive towards the target in an open cockpit machine and as the trigger was pressed to hear the violent chatter of the two Vickers guns positioned in front of his face. The guns had to be easily accessible because they were so prone to stoppages; consequently the pilots were trained to dismantle and to reassemble them. There was also a chance that a fault might develop in the Constantinesco synchronising gear, a device that was designed to prevent bullets striking the propeller. Sometimes they did.

Siskins of 29 Squadron, RAF. Bennett family

Those two weeks so pleasurably spent became a distant memory when a new flight commander was placed in authority over Bennett and his fellow pilots. "Never before or since", Bennett recalled, "have I met such a bureaucrat. Translating the orders of every other bureaucrat at higher levels as generously as he could, he produced every order in writing. He insisted upon signatures *ad nauseam* and reduced our flying both in frequency and duration." A training flight might be assigned with orders to the pilot to practise aerobatics above 6,000 feet and within 10 miles of North Weald, to be completed by a certain time. The flight commander would sign this instruction and demand a signature or initials in thirteen places. "All this", complained Bennett, "was intended to produce safety, the only ambition then existent in the RAF and the only basis on which promotions were judged."

The pilots fretted at such restrictions and considered applying for a posting to another squadron. One day the flight commander assigned formation flying practice to Bennett and another pilot called Widows, but forgot to write down his usual list of restrictions. "Grinning from ear to ear," as Bennett put it, "we agreed we would go somewhere and go we did." Bennett was the leader and he wanted to have a look at a place about sixty miles south of London. Dodging shower clouds which were present, he reached his chosen turning point and then wheeled round to fly home. To his consternation there now towered before him a formidable cold front with cloud down to low levels and hills to be flown over. The Siskin had no great range and the fuel remaining in the tanks did not permit any diversion from the direct track back to North Weald. Widows tucked alongside in close formation as Bennett entered the thick turbulent cloud. Very soon both aircraft gathered several inches of ice along the leading edge of the wings. A little later Bennett realised that his engine was losing power and then quite suddenly it stopped altogether. He saw Widows shoot past and disappear from sight into the clouds, and as his own aircraft silently descended he tightened his safety harness, switched off the ignition and turned off the fuel. When the aircraft broke cloud he was about 200 feet over a wood. There was a small field beyond the wood but only the barest possibility that the aircraft could reach it. Bennett heaved back the control stick to avoid the tops of the trees and the aircraft sank more rapidly. As the undercarriage struck the ground the Siskin pitched over and on to its back. He found himself inverted with his head only six inches from the ground but without a scratch, and he blessed the Sutton harness which had saved him from a broken neck. Widows arrived safely back at the aerodrome.

There was a formal inquiry which blamed the two pilots for flying so far south but took into consideration the absence of a forecast of weather bad enough to pose a threat of severe icing to their aircraft. Bennett accepted the blame but privately attributed his lack of concern about the weather to being regimented by a bureaucratic system which had deprived him of the opportunity to practise captaincy and airmanship. Later, when he was allowed to act as a real captain of an aircraft, he took the trouble to find out about the weather and to consider everything that he was doing.

When he had been a year with the squadron, Bennett applied for a course on flying boats. His aim was to obtain as much experience as possible on a wide variety of aircraft and it was an action that would prove to be of considerable importance to his future. The flying boat course was at Calshot, where a few hangars stood at the end of a spit of land extending into Southampton Water. The other pilots under instruction varied from squadron leaders to sergeant pilots and the course, half flying and half theory, lasted for six months. To Bennett, the change from a fighter to the heaviest of all the aircraft then operated by the RAF, the wooden-hulled Southampton, came as a considerable shock.

Of particular interest was the training in seamanship. The pupils not only learnt to handle the flying boat in the air and on water but also practised the art of picking up moorings and anchoring. Apart from flying, a large part of the course consisted of navigation instruction. It was customary for those associated with flying boats to use nautical terminology. They went aboard and ashore, moved forward and aft. Bennett's instructor was "a real old salt . . . he took great pride in the fact that the albatross on his cap badge was deep green from the salt sea spray". Bennett proved an apt pupil, and altogether it was a very happy six months.

His next posting was to 210 Squadron at Pembroke Dock. He loaded all his possessions into his aged Morris and drove across the Welsh mountains in pitch darkness and heavy rain illuminated at times by flashes of lighting. His first impressions of his new station were not welcoming—bleak empty streets and stone walls. Inded, the RAF station was completely surrounded by a high stone wall with one gate and seemed almost as desolate as a prison. Yet he was to find that Pembroke Dock was one of the happiest stations in the course of his service career. Very soon after his arrival he "had the pleasure of getting Bert Harris as our commanding officer and he certainly made things move". This was the man who a dozen years later was to become the Commander in Chief, Bomber Command.

The Southampton flying boats were soon replaced by the more modern Singapores. Night flying, formerly a rare activity for flying boats because of the problems of preparing a reasonably straight flare path, became a normal routine. Flying was carried out five miles down the estuary from Milford Haven where it was possible to obtain a sufficient take-off run in all directions. The squadron's

Supermarine Southampton. These entered RAF service in 1928. Bennett family

tasks included fishery protection patrols in co-operation with naval vessels, the object being to prevent French fishermen poaching inside British territorial waters. Other assignments did not always appear to serve any intelligible purpose. A six week long exercise in night flying, taking off from Dover Harbour and landing at Calshot, was "a most interesting occupation which had something to do with air defence."

Bennett was dismayed when this happy existence ended. His aptitude for navigation had resulted in his posting back to Calshot as an instructor in the navigation school. In addition to lecturing to the pilots who were attending the flying boat course he had an opportunity to take the specialist navigation course, an excellent basis for the civil First Class Navigator's Licence, which he ultimately obtained. Subsequently, he was transferred to instruct the pilots converting on to the flying boats; he was happiest when he was flying for a large part of the time. As an instructor he would set off with two or three pilot pupils, a wireless operator, a fitter, sometimes a rigger and a large amount of aircraft spares for about ten days. Night stops were made at RAF flying boat stations or at moorings known to be available at various harbours around the British Isles. Each day's flying would include a navigation exercise and perhaps anchoring trials at lunch times wherever they chose to

Supermarine Southampton alongside a RN submarine.
Bennett family

stop. Most of the time was spent in Scottish waters and the cruises were practised at all times of the year including the depths of winter.

"It was excellent for initiative", Bennett recalled. "We were often left very much to ourselves and if in trouble we had to take appropriate action entirely on our own initiative . . . being in open cockpit flying boats we were often drenched with spray or worse and it certainly taught me how to ignore the weather. Moreover engine failures were frequent and I had a good many forced landings in many odd places. These were sometimes fairly serious. The performance of a Southampton on one engine was rather like that of an overweight brick and therefore if an engine failure occurred over a heavy sea the result was generally fairly catastrophic. We never flew overland except for the shortest possible journeys."

Bennett was flying a Southampton over the English Channel on one occasion when one engine suddenly failed. He had just enough time to send out a signal announcing his imminent landing before he put down close to a Royal Navy destroyer cruising to the south of Portland Bill. The destroyer came alongside and offered a tow, which he gratefully accepted. A large steel hawser was soon attached to the very small bollard on the bow of the flying boat, then the destroyer set off at what Bennett considered to be far too fast a speed for the bollard to withstand. From the stern of the destroyer a sailor sent by semaphore the messsage "May we go faster?" Already considerably concerned he snapped to his signaller, "Certainly not!" The signaller, standing with semaphore flags on the aircraft's centre section, had got as far as "Certainly . . ." when the sailor disappeared from view. "In no time at all we were practically planing", Bennett later recalled; "never in my life have I seen a flying boat go so fast at the end of a piece of string as on that occasion." Riding so high and so fast over the sea the strain on the bollard was actually reduced, so Bennett allowed matters to continue. Very soon the aircraft was on a mooring in Portland Harbour. Then they changed the engine, as was their custom, with one fitter, three pupils, one instructor and one wireless operator . . . and no outside help.

*   *   *

On 1st January, 1934, the national newspapers reported that a Mr McRobertson was offering a large prize to the winner of an air race from England to Melbourne, to mark the Melbourne Centenary Celebrations. "I was keen to be in that race," Bennett confessed. "I knew something about navigation and had flown different types of aircraft but I had little to offer as a pilot in asking for some exceptional aircraft in which to compete. I decided therefore that I must get my First Class Navigator's Licence." He set to work at once to qualify for a licence which very few had yet obtained. The examinations were due to take place in March so his studies would demand a considerable proportion of his off-duty hours. The station commander at Calshot observed the custom of dressing for dinner five nights a week and these formal occasions were lengthy. Fortunately Bennett was able to get himself excused and studied every evening until two am each morning, stopping only to cook himself sausages on the open coal fire of his bedroom. His efforts were rewarded and he became the seventh holder of the licence in the world.

The attempt to secure an aircraft to fly in the race was less successful despite journeys, interviews and dashed hopes. When the closing date for entrants arrived, Bennett had to be satisfied with an offer by an Australian called Woods to act as his navigator in a single-engined Lockhead Vega monoplane. This was basically a good aeroplane but Woods had bought it second-hand and he lacked sufficient funds to have some very necessary modifications carried out. Nor was the aircraft ready in time to appear at Mildenhall aerodrome, the starting point, on the appointed day. Woods himself was not as concerned about this as his navigator and obtained permission over the telephone from the race committee to arrive a day late. There was a further problem when an undercarriage leg jammed solid and resisted all efforts to free it. Even this did not disturb Woods' tranquillity and he went to London to keep a social engagement, leaving Bennett and one mechanic to rectify the trouble. Although neither had ever seen a similar oleo-leg they took it apart, identified the problem and shortly before dawn had restored it, hopefully serviceable, to the aircraft. The Vega was then flown to Mildenhall with very little time left to prepare maps and compensate the compass. The very short range of the aeroplane meant frequent landings en route to refuel and added to the difficulty of winning a race dependent upon speed.

At 0639 on 20th October, 1934, Bennett and Woods were airborne from Mildenhall. Woods had not been able to raise enough money to equip the aircraft with radio, and as the first sector to Marseilles was flown almost continuously without a sight of the ground it was necessary to rely entirely upon dead reckoning. All went well and in under four hours they were safely on the ground; they refuelled and pressed on to Rome and then in the gathering darkness to Athens. Even with full tanks it was doubtful whether the Vega could reach Aleppo without refuelling, and as no night-flying facilities existed at any airfield in Cyprus, the two men decided to snatch a few hours' sleep. The Greek Air Force put them up in the local barracks and after a short rest they took off again. This time both Woods and Bennett were sure that the undercarriage leg had again jammed, and as Woods prepared to land at Aleppo, Bennett removed himself to the rear of the aircraft in the hope that this would keep the tail down. On landing, the Vega hit the ground "with a fair wallop" and the aircraft tipped over on to its back. Bennett was flung forward from the tail of the aircraft but was able to extricate himself from the machine and assisted Woods, who was bleeding profusely from his forehead.

The pilot turned out to be suffering fewer injuries than Bennett, who had suffered three crushed vertebrae, but they were both taken to a local convent where the Syrian nuns patched them up. The accident put them out of the race, which was won by Scott and Campbell-Black in a twin-engined de Havilland Comet, a machine which led to the development of the successful Mosquito. Woods waited for funds to be cabled from Australia so that he could repair his aircraft, while the British Air Attaché arrived and looked after Bennett before putting him on an American ship which sailed from Beirut to Alexandria and thereafter to Naples. Once on board, his acute bodily discomfort was increased by an ear infection which caused him a great deal of pain. Repeated efforts to see the ship's doctor proved fruitless, so finally, accompanied by

The accident that ended the attempt of Woods and Bennett to compete in the Mildenhall to Melbourne air race in a Lockheed Vega. Bennett family

one of the ship's officers, he let himself into the doctor's cabin to find him almost speechless from the effects of dope. With the officer's assistance he helped himself to whatever he believed might prove useful for his ear "and I survived", as he put it later.

A week later Bennett was back at Calshot, and with a stiff leg, three crushed vertebrae, an abscess in the ear and immobility of his head and shoulders he passed the annual medical examination. Many months passed before he could consider his backbone had recovered. Even so, within two weeks of the accident at Aleppo he was flying the Southampton with pupils on a training cruise.

During that autumn of 1934, Bennett met Ly, "a poor innocent girl from Switzerland" who was visiting England to improve her knowledge of the language. He was persistent in his approaches. As he wrote later, "Inevitably and inexorably I ultimately fell for the job of teaching her English and I have been doing it ever since."

Whilst at Calshot Bennett added to his navigator's licence the civil pilot's B Licence, an instructor's certificate, a ground engineer's licence in three categories and a wireless operator's licence, in preparation for the day when he would enter civil aviation. With this ambition in mind he did his best to keep in touch with landplanes; in 1933 he had paid £115 for a single-seater de Havilland 53, delightful to fly but ready to stall unless handled with care. More appropriate practice was obtained by offering his services unpaid at weekends to the newly established Jersey Airways, which operated de Havilland Dragons from Heston, Southampton and Portsmouth and used the beach at Jersey between tides as a landing ground. Bennett recognised as valuable experience the responsibility for his own paperwork, looking after the passengers and their baggage and managing singlehanded. It was sometimes a close run affair, departing from the beach before the tide rushed in, but no aircraft were ever engulfed, although the ancient bus driven to the beach and used as an office eventually was. This came to an end when a member of the House of Commons asked the Secretary of State for Air whether it was true that a regular RAF officer was depriving a civil pilot of his livelihood by flying for an airline.

In August, 1935, when Bennett had served at Calshot for several years, he left the RAF, but not with any sense of dissatisfaction, because he had enjoyed himself and felt greatly rewarded by the opportunities which had been presented to him. Rather, it appeared that he would be able to widen his experience elsewhere. He had logged 1,350 hours' flying on twenty-one different types, of which eight were marine aircraft.

Ten days after becoming a civilian again, he and Ly were married.

Bennett's first privately owned aircraft when he was a pilot officer.
Bennett family

Major Brackley, Air Superintendent of Imperial Airways in the 1930s. RAF Museum

Imperial Airways   2

YOUNG, recently married and unemployed, Bennett and Ly set off on a journey, first to Switzerland, so that he could be introduced to his bride's family and relations, and thereafter to Australia, where he would have the pleasure of showing off Ly to the Bennetts.

It was not in his nature, however, to let the grass grow under his feet. Before departing on this extended honeymoon Bennett had approached Imperial Airways with a view to his future employment as a civil pilot and astounded the personnel manager by producing the full range of civil licences which he had acquired. It was clear that the experience was new to the manager, who was at pains to conceal his eagerness to engage such a well qualified recruit.

He had also visited the publishers, Isaac Pitman, in London and offered to remedy the lack of any up to date manual on air navigation by writing a book himself. They expressed an interest and he began work on the ship to Australia. "It was a struggle", he wrote, "among passengers violently and aggressively engaged in a waste of time."

Bennett had not finally decided to return to England, and within a few weeks of his arrival in Brisbane he followed up another possible lead to an airline post. A finance house in London had purchased some aircraft for a company operating between Sydney and Brisbane, and armed with their letter of recommendation Bennett flew to Sydney to find out what possibilities lay within the country of his birth. The salary and the future prospects, however, appeared far less favourable than those in England so he decided to return. Owing to a strike which played havoc with the passenger ship schedules it was necessary for the Bennetts to return to England in a very slow cargo boat; at least there was no distraction by other passengers. By the time the ship docked in Southampton *The Complete Air Navigator* was ready for delivery to Pitman. It was to become the essential textbook for every aspirant to a First Class Navigator's Licence and revised editions continued to be published for the next thirty years.

In January, 1936, Bennett joined Imperial Airways whose Air Superintendent, Major Brackley, sent him to Croydon for a few weeks' training. A dozen years later Brackley was to replace Bennett as chief executive in another airline and the latter's comments upon him are interesting. He admired the Air Superintendent for his distinguished career in the First World War and for opening up the Empire routes to both Australia and South Africa. He strongly approved of Brackley's insistence that no airline official had the right to countermand any captain's decision to cancel a flight for reasons of weather or unserviceability of equipment. Finally "Brackley was largely responsible for the choice of aircraft, which were always of British construction, always thoroughly sound and reliable, and reasonably economical."

Very soon Bennett was rostered to fly as co-pilot on the Paris route in a Handley Page 42. It was a night service with a full load of passengers. The captain did not know that Bennett was a new recruit and after take-off went aft to talk to the passengers, only resuming his seat as the lights of Paris lay beneath the aircraft. Bennett was surprised to be left in charge of a large four-engined machine which was unfamiliar to him, and it came as a shock to the captain when he subsequently learnt that his co-pilot was making his first trip in that capacity.

Shortly thereafter, Bennett was sent to the company's flying boat base in Alexandria to operate the route to Athens and Brindisi. Brackley had assured him that he would be given a

Passengers boarding a Handley Page 42 at Croydon Airport.
British Airways

command and there was the added excitement at the possibility of promotion from the Kent *Scipio* cruising at seventy knots to the fleet of twenty eight Empire flying boats which had been ordered from Short Brothers. Meanwhile, because the salary structure of the airline was based on a very modest retainer plus a payment per hour flown, there was great rivalry to obtain an adequate share of the work. The loss of *Sylvanus*, which was burnt at its moorings during refuelling, reduced the workload further. It was replaced by an ancient open-cockpit Calcutta, whose slow speed and inadequate range sometimes obliged its pilot to turn back towards Alexandria when headwinds were encountered on the way to Brindisi. It was an irregular life, the crews never being sure where they would be spending the night as weather or servicing problems played havoc with the schedules. Obliged to spend five successive days in Brindisi, Bennett used the time profitably writing a complete book on the handling of flying boats, *The Air Mariner*.

The captain of a Handley Page 42 at the controls. British Airways

At the beginning of 1937, the first of the Empire flying boats was delivered and Imperial Airways decided to base the crews at Hythe, near Southampton. To his delight, Bennett was appointed to a command, and one of his first duties was to carry out fuel consumption tests around the British Isles. Characteristically, and against formidable opposition, he insisted on allowing two young signals clerks who worked in the airline's Hythe office to go on one such flight. Harry Pusey, now an aviation consultant, recalls that "throughout the flight he told us how everything functioned; allowed us to take drift sights both overland and over water; brought us our lunch and had his own with us; and acted as a perfect host-cum-scout-leader, cum-friendly-schoolmaster."

Very soon enough flying boats were delivered to allow them to operate through to Durban on the South African run and to Singapore on the Australian route. The Postmaster-General, Sir Kingsley Wood, simultaneously inaugurated the system by which all first class mail was carried throughout the British Commonwealth by air. All passenger aircraft of that era cruised below 10,000 feet and sometimes as low as 1,000 feet if there was no high ground to endanger the flight, the choice being determined by the weather and particularly the wind strength and direction. On the African route, it became customary to fly low enough for the passengers to see the Bor herd of elephants and the river below Murchison Falls which attracted so many hippo. There was a less enjoyable excitement for the radio officer whose job it was to attach the flying boat to the mooring buoy in the choppy river at Wadi Halfa. Crocodiles infested the muddy water and had already captured one unfortunate man who slipped from a refuelling barge.

Passengers are pleased to arrive on time at their destination;

The open cockpit of Shorts' Empire flying boat, delivered to the airline in 1928.
British Airways

few are particularly interested when they unwittingly become participants in a pilot's attempt to establish a record or claim a "first". When Bennett was in Alexandria waiting to take over an aircraft which had been delayed along the line he worked out that it might be possible to reach Southampton before dark and so pilot the first aircraft to fly from Egypt to England in one day. There were no facilities for a night landing at Southampton, so a very early start would have to be made. Not surprisingly there was grumbling from some of the passengers. They were often accommodated overnight on the ground in those days and were unenthusiastic at rising before first light. During the day, however, the success of the crew in reducing the time spent at refuelling stops engendered a response from the passengers. Landings had to be made at Athens, Brindisi, Bracciano and Marignane, near Marseilles. Headwinds had made Bennett fear that he might have to give up the attempt to reach Southampton and stop for the night at Marseilles. His enthusiasm, however, had proved infectious and by this time the passengers were sending the steward forward at increasingly short intervals to ask for progress reports. To the delight of all on board, they arrived at Hythe with twenty minutes' daylight remaining.

Although the Empire flying boats had proved to be a great success they did not have the range to operate across the Atlantic ocean with any worthwhile load. By 1938, Pan American Airways were preparing to inaugurate an Atlantic service using their Boeing flying boat, whilst American Export Airlines proposed to introduce the Sikorsky flying boat. The Germans were experimenting with a catapult device to propel a flying boat from a ship after it had landed alongside to take on fuel. Bennett was involved in two separate experiments conducted by Imperial Airways to investigate the feasibility of air travel across the North Atlantic.

The first of these experiments, sponsored by the Air Ministry, was the *Mercury-Maia* composite. Major Mayo, Technical Manager of Imperial Airways, held the patents for the technical mechanism of the composite which was designed and built by Short Brothers. *Mercury* was a small four-engined monoplane on floats into which could be stowed mail and freight. The tiny fuselage had cockpit space for one pilot and one wireless operator. This little machine was mounted above *Maia*, which was a modified Empire flying boat. The basic principle was that with all eight engines at full throttle the amount of power from the lightly laden *Maia* would bear the main burden of lifting *Mercury* from the surface until level flight was achieved. *Mercury* would then be released and be able to take its load across the Atlantic.

Bennett's formal application early in 1938 for the command of *Mercury* had been accepted but he became increasingly exasperated

by the delays at Felixstowe, where the aircraft was being tested by the government establishment. Moreover, despite Major Mayo's senior status and his fine intellect, his meek and mild manner was not such as to spur a sense of urgency among the Felixstowe staff. "I really think", wrote Bennett, "that if I had not been present during the whole of the tests they might have taken two years or more to complete them." The North Atlantic had never been flown in winter so obviously the flight for which the aircraft had been designed must take place during the summer. This season was well advanced when *Mercury* and *Maia* were finally released to the airline's base in Southampton Water. Two test flights, each with its traumatic moments, preceded the main event. In the first of these Bennett had reached the upper surface of *Maia* just before entering *Mercury* when he slipped on an oily patch and fell into the sea, still clutching his sextant, chronometer and other essential items. Stripping and changing into a ground engineer's overall, he carried on the test flight as arranged. The second test might have been ruined by the failure of the inter-communication system between Bennett and the captain of *Maia*, Wilcockson. Despite this the separation was achieved and the test went ahead.

There was another hurdle—bureaucracy—before the projected flight could go ahead. Along with Mayo and Wilcockson, Bennett attended a meeting called by the Air Ministry. He always remembered how "Lashings of civil servants, some said to be scientific, some admittedly not, sat around and told us that *Mercury*

Mercury *with* Maia *attached.*
British Airways

21

with a full load of petrol could barely do the trip to Botwood in Newfoundland and that its return flight without *Maia* to help it was quite impossible." Bennett observed that the reaction of Mayo, "a somewhat sensitive man, was to shrivel up and disappear." It remained for Bennett to point out that the civil servants' calculations were based on fuel consumption tests on rich mixture. Then "they gracefully stood aside and let us continue the projected flights."

The departure point was to be Foynes on the River Shannon in the Irish Republic. There the newspapers, cinema films and other packages, a half ton in all and the first commercial load to be carried across the North Atlantic, were stowed in the floats. On 20th July, 1938, Bennett separated with *Mercury* from *Maia* and accompanied by Radio Officer Coster began the long journey towards Canada. Because headwinds were forecast he reduced his altitude after the separation and while daylight lasted cruised for several hours at about fifty feet above the surface of the sea. Fortunately, the aircraft was fitted with a good automatic pilot and a reliable compass. Alongside his seat were his sextant, slide rule and pencils, while his chart board lay on his lap. Bennett climbed to 500 feet as darkness fell and encountered heavy rain and turbulence as he flew through a warm front. When the winds veered from the west to become northerly he climbed to a more fuel-economical height, and clear skies enabled him to obtain star sightings and thus to plot his position on his chart. Exactly on flight plan time and on track he was able to fix his position as he caught a glimpse of the island in the strait of Belle Isle through the broken clouds below. He decided that it would be possible to continue the flight to Montreal without refuelling at Botwood in Newfoundland. It was fine and sunny when he landed and moored up; the flight across the ocean had taken twenty hours and twenty minutes. *Mercury* was then refuelled and the journey was continued to New York.

The official welcome by the Minister for Transport at Montreal had been spoiled for Bennett by the horde of pressmen and photographers, whom he greatly offended by declining to give interviews until he had completed formalities with the authorities. But this was nothing compared with his reception in New York, of which Bennett said, "I had seen displays by Australian aboriginals in which they reach a climax of frenzy by rushing, shaking shields, spears, woomeras violently . . . instead of Abos we had cameramen and instead of spears, cameras with flash bulbs. Never have I seen anything like it. Even the full size newspapers carried photographs of *Mercury* over the whole width of the front page."

The return flight, which required *Mercury* to use only its own power, restricted its fuel load to one third of capacity, so Bennett

flew home by way of Botwood, the Azores and Lisbon. Sir Kingsley Wood, recently transferred to the post of Secretary of State for Air, received him, and this provided Bennett with an opportunity to ask for official approval for an attempt on the world's long distance seaplane record. The current record of about 4,500 miles had been set only six months earlier by a German seaplane which had been catapulted from a ship. Sir Kingsley showed interest and Bennett then broached the subject with Mayo and the managing director of Imperial Airways, Woods Humphery. Bennett had envisaged a flight from Southampton to Cape Town, but his success in crossing the Atlantic had transformed the earlier pessimists into unyielding optimists. Accordingly, he was urged to attempt the world's absolute record and not merely the seaplane record. Modifications were made to *Mercury* so that the floats could serve as fuel tanks and electric pumps were fitted to pump the petrol up to the wing tank

Paul Bewshea, Imperial Airways' man in New York (wearing the double-breasted suit) introduces Captain Bennett and Radio Officer Coster to the Press, following their arrival in Mercury.
Bennett family

when needed. As a precaution, a hand pump was also added. In order to achieve the necessary distance for the world record the starting point was to be Dundee. In place of Coster a former wireless operator called Harvey was chosen to accompany Bennett, as he had recently qualified as a pilot.

Bennett had hoped to make the flight in September, 1938, but the Czechoslovakian crisis intervened and the Air Ministry ordered a delay. The Munich pact disgusted Bennett and he was not impressed by the evident relief of the officers in the RAF Mess at Leuchars where he was staying. He confessed that "For the first time in my life I was thoroughly ashamed of a British action."

A different view about the postponement of hostilities with Germany was held by a former director of British Airways, Harold Balfour, who had been appointed by Churchill to be deputy to Sir Kingsley Wood early that summer. After the war he was to write, "In September, 1938, the Luftwaffe could have shot the RAF out of the skies with their well armed high performance monoplanes." Balfour had been appalled to learn how unprepared were Britain's defences. The seventeen new stations intended to provide radar coverage from Newcastle to Land's End were not completed. Nineteen of the regular fighter squadrons were still equipped with biplanes and only two with Hawker Hurricanes; there were not enough Supermarine Spitfires to equip a single squadron. He concluded: "We did our best in the year left to us and I say, 'Thank God for Munich'."

War averted, the Air Ministry authorised the departure of Bennett but he had to wait for days for a forecast which did not predict strong headwinds for at least the first 1,000 miles. On 6th October, it was decided to go before the weather deteriorated. The composite had not before made a take-off at the weight required on this occasion but the climb and release were successful except for the loss of one of *Mercury's* cowlings, which tore off in the slipstream. When Bennett became aware of this mishap, the effect of which was to increase the drag on the aircraft and thus increase fuel consumption, he had to decide whether to continue. But even if he jettisoned fuel it would still take twelve hours to reduce the aircraft's weight sufficiently for a safe landing. He made up his mind to continue the flight because a return to Dundee could have induced the authorities to cancel the attempt upon the record.

Over the south of England, icing in cloud made it necessary to reduce height. The important task was fuel conservation and Bennett kept a log of fuel consumption, plotting this every half hour and calculating his ground miles flown per gallon used, while Harvey sent position reports by radio to London. Once the Atlas mountains in northern Africa had been crossed, the weather over the Sahara was perfect. Bennett's impeccable navigation enabled him to maintain his chosen track and he was feeling more optimistic after passing Kano in northern Nigeria, although hopes of surpassing the absolute distance record were fading. Then a problem arose: the petrol pumps fitted to lift fuel from the floats to the wing tank failed to function. Harvey had to combine his radio duties with attempts to rectify the pump fault and when his efforts proved unsuccessful, to operate the hand pump. For reasons of fuel economy a cruising level of about 13,000 feet had been reached and lack of oxygen made pumping a strenuous activity. Bennett relieved Harvey from time to time, but as the flight progressed thunderstorms, heavy turbulence and torrential rain obliged him to remain at the controls. Unless the remaining fuel in the floats could be pumped into the main tank it might not be possible to stay airborne throughout the second night. They were flying over land and there were no seaplane stations along the coast; it would thus be impossible to ask for night landing facilities. Bennett and Harvey worked like Trojans to pump fuel but as darkness fell there was still insufficient in the main tank to last the night. Harvey's continuous exertions and the lack of oxygen rendered him ineffective for a period; he began to have hallucinations and Bennett had to rely on the automatic pilot and concentrate on the pumping.

Without any radio assistance on the second night, Bennett was totally dependent upon his sextant for establishing the aircraft's position. As dawn approached he had the satisfaction of knowing that the existing world's seaplane record had been broken, although he was not going to be able to reach Cape Town. At daybreak they were flying over South West Africa and Bennett decided to head for Alexander Bay on the Orange River, which was within the borders of the Union of South Africa. The wobble pump was sucking air but they kept working it in the hope that any remaining fuel would be brought up. There was very little reading on the fuel gauges when Bennett put *Mercury* down in the estuary of the river mouth at the end of forty-two and a half hours' flight, a new world's long distance record of 6,000 miles. During the whole of this time the young signals clerk Harry Pusey and his colleague insisted on remaining on duty to keep track of Bennett's progress. As Pusey put it, "I suppose we felt partly responsible for him."

After refuelling, *Mercury* was flown on to Cape Town, where Bennett and Harvey received a great reception. Their main regret was that they had not started from Southampton instead of Dundee and thereby been able to make their first landing at Cape Town. After two enjoyable days, Bennett flew *Mercury* to the Imperial Airways base at Durban and then a more leisurely flight was undertaken to England.

The autumn chill of late October was matched by Bennett's

comments upon the reaction at home to his achievement. "After this flight, which was one of the world's major air records, I received no offical reception, no trace of recognition of any sort from the government, and no celebrations from Imperial Airways or from Napiers, the makers of the engines. I wonder if such a flight could have occurred in any other country without at least some form of celebration on the return."

In November, *Mercury* was ready for the next task, to inaugurate the first commercial non-stop service to Egypt, carrying about a ton of first-class mail. Accompanying Bennett and Radio Officer Coster on the flight was a ground engineer, Donald Munro, who had been associated with the composite project since its inception and had been responsible for servicing *Mercury* upon its arrival in South Africa and at each stage of the journey home. He was being carried to Alexandria on a temporary posting. "Captain Bennett's technical competence," he recalls, "was of a very high standard, in fact much greater than my own. But he always respected my opinion and was an easy person to please if one did one's job properly."

The temperature within *Mercury* was bitterly cold, there being no provision for cockpit heating, but this did not seem to bother Bennett. He had engaged the autopilot and was busily navigating by means of astrofixes, the Mediterranean being entirely covered by cloud and without any landmarks visible. Fourteen hours after their departure from England, Bennett turned to Munro and said, "When war comes, accurate bombing of targets in Germany will depend upon precise navigation. I have conducted the flight with this in mind and should we now release a bomb it would target Ras-El-Tin immediately ahead and below us." Then he closed the throttles and banked the aircraft in a left hand turn to descend through the cloud cover. As *Mercury* broke through the lowest layer, Munro observed Alexandria harbour and the Imperial Airways base at Ras-El-Tin directly beneath the aircraft.

At the end of the winter the flights of *Mercury* to North America were not resumed. The Air Ministry had funded the project but now decided not to continue it as they were opposed to an exclusive mail carrier and wanted an aircraft which could carry passengers as well as cargo.

In the late Spring of 1939, Imperial Airways embarked upon a new experiment leading towards the introduction of a trans-Atlantic service. This required the co-operation of Sir Alan Cobham and his staff of Flight Refuelling Ltd. An Empire flying boat was modified so that a pipe was let out from the tail section. This was picked up by the tanker aircraft, a converted Handley Page Harrow bomber, winched in and connected to its supply. The tanker then pumped fuel through the pipe to the flying boat.

Bennett was selected to take part in the programme together with Captain Gordon Store and Captain Kelly Rogers.

In August, the inaugural two way service began. Kelly Rogers set out from New York and was refuelled by the aircraft which Cobham had stationed in Newfoundland, while Bennett took off from Southampton and landed at Foynes. After leaving Foynes, he was met by the refuelling aircraft and enjoyed an uneventful flight of sixteen and a half hours to Botwood and thereafter to Montreal and New York. The height at which refuelling was carried out was about 1,000 feet. Once, because of low cloud, refuelling was conducted above the treetops. About fifteen trans-Atlantic crossings were made, but not altogether without incident. On one occasion contact between the tanker and the flying boat was prematurely broken and fuel lost. A further problem was the lack of any alternative airport to Botwood other than Moncton 500 miles away. Flight refuelling with passengers on board seemed a remote solution.

During that last summer before the outbreak of the Second World War Imperial Airways was amalgamated with British Airways and the Conservative government decided that the airline should operate as a public corporation under the title British Overseas Airways Corporation. This decision and the events which preceded it, involving the removal of Woods Humphery, managing director of Imperial Airways, caused bitter resentment among many of those who had worked under him. Years later, Bennett was to write, "This act was in my view one of the most remarkable pieces of political nonsense that I have ever seen. Imperial Airways had been created as part of government policy to run the overseas routes of the Empire and was technically and operationally most successful. For the Empire mail scheme it received a small subsidy but otherwise had no aid at all. Beside our airline there had grown up a small company operated principally by people who were critics of Imperial Airways . . . it seemed to me that they used almost entirely foreign aircraft—Dutch, German and American—without ever operating British aircraft on a regular basis . . . More serious however was that the technical heads of the small company were given the key positions in the new corporation. Moreover the pioneers of the Empire air routes were given no recognition whatever. Woods Humphery left Great Britain and went to live abroad as a direct result of this unhappy political viciousness and never returned. Neither he nor Major Mayo ever received any honours for the grand pioneering work they had done. Imperial Airways was at that time the major airline of the world, its machines were almost entirely the four engined aircraft it had itself pioneered; it covered half the world with its routes. The merry men of Major Brackley, the Air Superintendent, had seared

A Handley Page Harrow refuels the Shorts' Empire flying boat Cabot *over Southampton Water in 1939.* RAF Museum

their way through Darkest Africa and across the deserts of the world and had brought civilisation and good communications to all sorts of outposts of the Empire . . . it is as deplorable as it is typical that the country of their birth gave them no honour."

In view of what was to happen less than ten years later, when Bennett was to be the first chief executive of British South American Airways with responsibilities which included aircraft procurement, these comments about the circumstances of the creation of BOAC deserve examination. It was only natural that Bennett should express loyalty towards the employer in whose service he had gained such distinction, but he was very fortunate to have had the opportunity to fly the Short Empire flying boat, one of the few currently successful British designs. Major Mayo had prepared the specification and the order for twenty-eight had been placed in 1935. Short Brothers had wanted to build a prototype because of the design innovations, but were urged to go into production as quickly as possible. The first aircraft flew in 1936 and deliveries followed during each sucessive month; proving flights were few and some of the aircraft were handed over with only one

The passenger cabin of Shorts' Kent class flying boat. It carried sixteen passengers across the Mediterranean at 105 mph. Three were built for Imperial Airways in 1931 and were known as "Scipio" types.
RAF Museum

flight by the manufacturers recorded in the aircraft log book. Passenger services began in 1937 and the popularity and success of this flying boat attracted orders from other airlines.

In other respects however the reputation of Imperial Airways had suffered, although the reasons for this lay to some extent outside its own responsibility. As the "chosen instrument" of the British government it was under an obligation to fly British manufactured aircraft, a condition which Bennett clearly approved. The consequences of this policy involved penalties. The Armstrong Whitworth Ensign ordered in 1934 had not been delivered until the end of 1938 and then had to be withdrawn from passenger service for modifications. The same fate befell the de Havilland Albatross and the airline had been forced to continue to fly the 1931 vintage Heracles class. Safe and reliable as the old landplanes were, they were slower than those of their European rivals and uncompetitive.

During 1936, four small British private companies had united to form British Airways, in which all the shares were held by private interests. The government had no financial stake in the new company but aware of the intense concentration by Imperial Airways in the development of the Empire routes, had responded to pressure for improved air services in Europe by adopting the newcomer as their second "chosen instrument" and according it a subsidy. Whereas Imperial Airways was under an obligation to operate British aircraft, no such restrictions were imposed on British Airways. The rearmament programme had started and aircraft manufacturers were fully engaged in the production of military aircraft; they could not accord any priority to civil designs. Consequently, British Airways bought Fokker aircraft from Holland, Junkers 52s from Germany and Lockheed Electras from the United States in a bid to compete with their European rivals on routes to Paris, Berlin and Warsaw.

Mr Robert Perkins, MP. He asked for a public inquiry on the conduct of Imperial Airways in 1938.
Sir Mark Norman

"Political nonsense" was certainly evident as a consequence of the government's actions. Paying a subsidy to each of the "chosen instruments" to compete with each other on the same routes meant that the taxpayer was paying out his money with both hands. Woods Humphery soon found himself at the centre of a storm with many different elements but which fundamentally rested on the need to decide whether the function of Imperial Airways was to operate at a profit or to uphold the prestige of Great Britain as the national airline. Two Conservative members of parliament led the attack on the company: Robert Perkins, who declared the airline's service in Europe to be "the laughing stock of the world . . . operated by obsolete aircraft" and Moore Brabazon, one of the first Englishmen to hold a pilot's licence, who became well known as Lord Brabazon of Tara.

The Cadman committee set up by the government made Woods Humphery the scapegoat. Sir John Reith, who had been chairman of the BBC, was appointed full time chairman of Imperial Airways and it made good sense to him that since British Airways also depended upon a government subsidy, a non-commercial constitution was required for British civil aviation. The outcome was the merger of Imperial Airways and British Airways into the British Overseas Airways Corporation, a nationalised concern.

The manner of effecting the resignation of Woods Humphery offended not only Bennett but many of the airline's captains and indeed almost all the long-serving staff of Imperial Airways. They were also dismayed by the departure of others among their chiefs, for appointed to the Board of BOAC were several directors of British Airways. One was Clive Pearson, their chairman, who became deputy to Reith, another was Gerard D'Erlanger, who was to become chairman of BOAC during the 1950s.

Ironically, Reith and Woods Humphery were old friends who had once worked at adjoining desks in the drawing office of a locomotive works in Glasgow. But the former was insistent that the

airline's long-serving managing director should not be offered a place on the board of BOAC. He acknowledged the value of the work he had done but criticised his style of administration. "It was a profound shock", he wrote, "to find in a concern of this size that it depended upon one individual . . . without Woods Humphery no one knew where they were . . . in later years he accused me of smashing up his organisation, the organisation in fact which I had not been able to find."

The mudslinging at the airline in which he took so much pride and to which he had given such loyalty undoubtedly coloured the attitude of Bennett towards BOAC. Its subsequent history as a political football and recipient of government ordained directives, coupled with growing financial losses and the abandonment of the Buy-British policy, made him more convinced than ever that the state was not competent to be trusted with the industry which he loved so much.

The reorganisation of the airline during the summer of 1939 took place against the far more sombre background of the approach of war in Europe. On 3rd September, 1939, Mrs Bennett drove her husband from their home in Dibden Purlieu in the New Forest to the flying boat base at Hythe. There was still time after signing the ship's papers and studying the weather charts to listen to the Prime Minister, Neville Chamberlain, as he broadcast to the nation that Great Britain was at war with Germany. Bennett found his words profoundly uninspiring. "In this grave hour he made no soul-stirring appeal to the people of Great Britain. He simply declared war."

There was no reason why the flight to North America, almost the last of the series, should not proceed as planned. The first stage to Foynes was completed and flight refuelling was carried out after the departure from Ireland. As darkness fell, the radio officer handed Bennett a message which he had heard transmitted. It was the SOS of the liner *Athenia*, torpedoed en route to the United States with almost a thousand passengers on board. There was nothing he could do except relay *Athenia*'s messages and continue the flight.

The war brought a reorganisation of the airline's routes. Bennett was put on special duties in connection with enemy submarines, a task which he found exciting at times and on which he was engaged until the spring of 1940, when he returned to route flying. He was on a flight from Singapore and had landed at Lake Bracciano near Rome on the day in June on which Mussolini decided to enter the war. Bennett evacuated the English staff of the airline and then flew on to St Nazaire, where they stayed overnight. "The place was full of dispute and despondency", he recalled. "It was the last time I saw St Nazaire intact."

Opposite page, above:
Lieutenant Colonel Moore-Brabazon, MP (later Lord Brabazon of Tara), who supported Robert Perkins in his criticism of Imperial Airways.
Lord Brabazon of Tara

Below: *Left to Right, Major Mayo, Major Woods Humphery and Lieutenant Colonel Burchall on the occasion of Woods Humphery's departure from Imperial Airways in 1939*
British Airways

Back at Hythe, Bennett had also to part with *Mercury*. It was a melancholy occasion, as he had been its only operating pilot. He flew it to Felixstowe and thereafter it was used for reconnaissance work by 320 Squadron before being scrapped in August 1941.

A few days later Bennett was to return to France again, where by now Marshal Pétain had capitulated to the Germans. The leader of the Polish government-in-exile, General Sikorski, had returned from the continent and asked Winston Churchill for assistance in rescuing members of his cabinet and staff whom he knew to be in the area of Bordeaux. Troops were still being evacuated through the port so the risk was considered to be acceptable. Bennett was given the job of taking General Sikorski and some aides to Biscarosse, south of Bordeaux, and his orders were to do everything possible to assist the general, but under no circumstances to permit the loss of the flying boat. "It was one of those very convenient orders", he recalls, "with two conflicting requirements."

Flying the Empire boat *Cathay* he put down at Biscarosse at midday. A dinghy was put over the side and the Poles went ashore. Bennett had stressed the risk of spending more than a few hours in the area but Sikorski replied that he could not be ready to leave before five o'clock the following morning; he also produced a letter bearing Winston Churchill's signature. Bennett therefore agreed to wait until first light, after which he would definitely take off and fly home. Meanwhile, he was faced with the problem of concealing a large flying boat for seventeen hours in exposed waters and liable to enemy attack. Accordingly he taxied *Cathay* along the coast for six miles and ran her lightly aground on a sandy beach under cover of some trees, turning her with a burst of engine power in order that she should come to rest facing open water.

During the afternoon enemy aircraft flew over and air bombardment in the area was heard. Bennett made contact by telephone with the seaplane station at Biscarosse and learned that German mobile columns were active, gathering in French Servicemen. The local people also warned him to keep out of sight as tanks had already passed through the village street. Bennett returned to the flying boat, and as darkness fell he started the engines and taxied back to the original moorings. Given the evidence of enemy activity, Bennett did not expect to see Sikorski again. At first light there was still no sign of him and the flying boat crew were becoming very anxious. Bennett took the dinghy ashore for a last look and at that moment four cars appeared, packed with Poles including Sikorski's daughter. Bennett started the engines as soon as all were aboard and headed out west to clear the coast as rapidly as possible. Moments after take-off, the crew looked down on the startled faces of a German tank crew refuelling near the Biscarosse base. Bennett had told the Poles to smash an aircraft window and

Crew of Caribou *at Quebec, Canada, on 6th September, 1939, after arriving from Port Washington, New York.* Trans-Canada Air Lines, courtesy Mr Cheesman

shoot at anything which posed a threat to the aircraft but recalled, "The only thing that shot at us was a British cruiser just off the estuary . . . fortunately the shooting was more or less of their usual standard and we were not hit." They flew over damaged and deserted ships and looked down upon lifeboats containing the bodies of dead men. A vast column of black smoke which rose from the oil storage tanks at Ushant provided a useful cover. Bennett successfully avoided German fighters and delivered his distinguished passengers to a welcoming party which awaited them at Poole harbour. As for the airline's own staff there, he found "they did not know exactly what our job had been but seemed surprised that we had returned."

One week later in early July, 1940, Bennett was assigned quite a different task. This was to carry the Duke of Kent to an international exhibition in Lisbon. He and his crew found it a strange experience to be accommodated at the same hotel as that used by the German airline crews. The return flight was begun at night from the Tagus river, the navigation lights being extinguished as they flew out of the estuary and northwards towards the British Isles to land at dawn in Poole harbour. This was the last occasion on which Bennett commanded an aircraft of the British Overseas Airways Corporation.

Today only a few elderly residents and a small number of aviation enthusiasts can point out the remains of the former flying boat base. Anyone driving along Shore Road, Hythe, and along Roman Road, Dibden Purlieu, can observe through the gates of what was Imperial Airways a two storey corrugated iron building and the windows of Bennett's office as deputy to Captain Wilcockson.

The Atlantic Ferry Organisation   3

THE FORMER General Manager of Imperial Airways, Woods Humphery, had gone to the United States a few months after his resignation and was occupied there with a business of his own. Following the outbreak of the war he urged the British Purchasing Commission that the Lockheed aircraft ordered for the RAF should be flown across the Atlantic rather than take up valuable space in ships and risk being lost through torpedo attack in the course of the slow and dangerous voyage to Britain. In July, 1940, when the possibility of a German invasion was occupying everyone's minds, this idea was adopted.

The newspaper proprietor Lord Beaverbrook was Winston Churchill's choice as Minister for Aircraft Production, and he set about this task with zeal. Disregarding the British Purchasing Commission and without waiting for Cabinet approval, Beaverbrook not only appointed his own buying agent but pledged British funding without reserve. Morris Wilson, the President of the Royal Bank of Canada, was the man invested with the Minister's own very considerable powers; Woods Humphery was appointed as his deputy; Canadian Pacific Railways were made responsible for the despatch of the aircraft from Canada.

Bennett was delighted to be chosen, along with two other pilots, Page and Ross, to form part of the Atlantic Ferry Organisation. At a time when the war news was all bad he was encouraged by the impression of energy and urgency shown by Beaverbrook when they met. He was impatient to have something important to do. He had a great respect for Woods Humphery and found that his colleague Captain Wilcockson would also be involved. Another flying boat pilot who had left BOAC to join the Royal Canadian Air Force was detached to assist operations; this was "Taffy" Powell, subsequently an Air Commodore and after the war an airline operator.

Bennett's enthusiasm was tempered by his unfavourable impression of Morris Wilson, and his comments upon him were succinct. "No doubt he must have been a very capable man, but so far as I was concerned I can only say that I have never met anyone so devoid of qualities either good or bad."

Bennett was Flying Superintendent, Wilcockson was Superintendent of Operations. Powell wrote, "an overlap of responsibility

Opposite page:
Captain Wilcockson and Captain Bennett.
Bennett family

can be read into these two similar titles and it was certainly true at the time because Bennett had great technical knowledge and was capable of working an eighteen hour day but in the process was somewhat abrasive. The two men were not cast in the same mould".

Bennett's first task was to visit the Lockheed works in California, manufacturers of the twin engined Hudson bombers that were to be the first aircraft to be flown to Britain. He and Page were hospitably received but their hosts were taken aback when he demanded a test flight first thing in the morning with himself at the controls and in charge of readings. He recalled that "This caused considerable consternation, as they had anticipated that I would be happy to sit and watch and accept the figures which they produced . . . by first thing I meant first light and this again caused consternation." Bennett was enabled to carry out a five hour test and satisfied himself that the Hudson was inferior to the claimed performance by about eight per cent and therefore that extra fuel would be required for the Atlantic crossing. Although at first the Lockheed technicians were inclined to doubt his figures, Bennett gave them full credit for accepting both these and his own analysis of the reasons for the shortfall in performance. Not only was his request for extra fuel granted but the following day the test aircraft had been fitted with an extra tank in the fuselage. The speed with which this was done and the wonderful spirit of co-operation was an object lesson that he would not forget, and he expressed the wish that "some British manufacturers could get the idea into their heads that the customer is sometimes right."

Bennett and Page accompanied the first two Hudsons to be delivered to Canada. Legal and diplomatic regulations did not permit them to fly the aircraft themselves; the United States was still neutral and the American pilots were careful to remain "on the beam" as they passed over one radio beacon and altered course towards the next one, even if it meant flying through thunderstorms. Bennett was not impressed by this routine manner of navigation in North America. Eventually, a landing was made at Pembina on the Canadian border. When the engines had been stopped, a horse was hitched on to the front of each aircraft to tow it across the border, and this formality avoided any breach of the American Neutrality Act. The two American pilots were in no great hurry to reach Montreal and a night stop at Kapuskasing in an area of great scenic beauty would, Bennett felt, have gratified anyone in a mood to enjoy it.

There was an urgent need to recruit pilots and wireless operators competent to fly the Hudsons to Britain. Beaverbrook had authorised the British authorities in Washington to offer very high rates of pay to volunteers who proved acceptable, and the applicants included bush pilots, crop-dusters, sky writers, barn-

stormers and enthusiastic amateurs; there were also men who had for one reason or another been ejected from the airlines. This policy caused considerable friction and dissatisfaction among the pilots sent over from Britain or arriving from as far away as Australia. Bennett went on record as declaring that all the necessary pilots and probably better ones could have been acquired without "this pathetic piece of bribery". Powell took a different view. Referring to the thousand dollars a month on offer, he wrote "They were fair rates for the job, which had none of the advantages of service life with accommodation found, care provided during illness and a pension at the end." The RAF could spare no pilots but BOAC sent a dozen, including Gordon Store and David Brice. Both men were after the war to be associated with Bennett again.

Experienced air wireless operators were also required, and they had almost ceased to exist. The American and Canadian airlines no longer employed them because, as Bennett had observed, the pilots had for many years been "riding the range", the routes clearly defined by audible radio stations. Within Canada, wireless operators who had worked for Marconi or the Canadian Department of Transport were invited to apply for training. Most were keen, with a good standard of Morse but little idea of geography and less experience of flying. These were the men

The first Lockheed Hudson delivered by air to the RAF. It had to land in North Dakota and be towed across the border to comply with the US Neutrality Act.
State Historical Society of North Dakota

Above: *Captain Gordon Store of Imperial Airways, who took part in the North Atlantic trials of the Empire boats in 1938. He joined Bennett on the ferry service in 1940 and was operations manager of BSAA in 1946.* G. Store

Below: *B-24 Liberators used to ferry flight crews across the North Atlantic.* British Airways

whose first long flight was to be the trans-Atlantic crossing. One of them wrote, "We knew we were to fly Hudsons across the Atlantic but none of us had seriously thought about it until the day Captain Bennett walked into the radio shack and sat down at the key and gave us all a test. By this time I had ceased to marvel and it seemed only natural that he should check out radio men as well as pilots and navigators. The next day there were a lot of faces missing and we came to realise that those of us still there had been chosen."

Bennett left it to Page and Ross to train the selected pilots on the first two Hudsons whilst he returned to California. The first of the long range Hudsons would be ready for delivery by mid-September, and thereafter fifty had been promised within two months. The object of his journey on this occasion was to visit another manufacturer, Consolidated, and to inspect a four engined bomber later to become known as the "Liberator", the prototype of which was flying within eleven months from the drawing board stage. Bennett was greatly impressed by this achievement and by the considerable range and payload claimed for the aircraft; it struck him at once that it could be adapted to carry passengers. He had in mind the urgent need to bring back the Hudson delivery crews after each flight to Britain.

He also flew the small twin engined flying boat which entered service with the RAF Coastal Command as the "Catalina". The first of these was delivered to Montreal, but the St Lawrence river freezes in winter and subsequent flights would have to use an alternative route. Bennett sent Ross to California for the second boat with instructions to fly it across the Southern States to Bermuda and thence direct to Britain. Ross was the first pilot in the Atlantic Ferry Organisation to fly an American aircraft across the Atlantic.

By October, 1940, a small number of Hudsons had been flown to Gander in preparation for the first delivery flight. This airfield was still in process of construction by the Newfoundland government in association with the Air Ministry. It lay on a remote tract of land that had been cleared of lumber following its selection as a North American terminal during the 1930s, when long range planning for future commercial operations across the Atlantic had begun. Originally known as Hattie's Camp, it took the name of Gander from a nearby lake. In 1938, a signals unit was stationed there. By the autumn of 1940, in addition to a good runway there was a team of meteorologists, but living accommodation was almost non-existent. To provide quarters for the flight crews some sleeping cars and a dining car wre made available by the Newfoundland Railway and placed on a siding near the solitary hangar.

The North Atlantic had never been flown in winter, and the project now about to begin was regarded by many of the authorities involved as a dangerous venture risking such severe losses of aircraft that it might have to be abandoned. The first menace was that of storms, whose violence would cause aircraft to buck and bounce and the engines to cough and splutter. Secondly, the direction and strength of winds could never be predicted with enough confidence to permit the use of forecasts as reliable guides to navigation. Winter fog was a constant hazard, liable to shroud an airfield without much warning. Without any doubt, however, the greatest concern to every airman centred upon ice, which was a killer and acted upon aircraft in various ways. The pilot's air speed indicator might show a gradual loss of speed, and if he could see the leading edge of his wings he might notice that ice had formed along its length. He would then have to decide whether to try to climb above the cloud level and risk the aircraft stalling if the speed continued to decrease, or to descend and hope that he could find warmer air below the freezing level to thaw the ice already accumulated.

In an attempt to combat one hazard, Pan American Airways were among the first to have rubber "shoes" fitted to the wing leading edge to dislodge ice at an early stage in its formation. In Britain the airlines had adopted a device of the railwaymen, who used a yellow paste called "Kilfrost" to try to prevent the points along the track from freezing. Bennett had this smeared along the unprotected edges of the wings and tailplane. Yet ice could also form in the carburettors, causing engines to lose power, on propellers, reducing their efficiency, and on the fuselage so that the weight of the aircraft was increased and its aerodynamic performance diminished. Freezing rain falling on an aircraft could force it down.

At the beginning of November, Bennett was almost ready to take the first of the Hudsons to Britain. He had satisfied himself that the selected pilots and wireless operators were competent, but the almost total lack of qualified navigators had obliged him to adopt the policy of a formation flight across the ocean. Each of the initial seven aircraft was fitted with station-keeping lights visible from behind, and instructions were given to pilots on the procedure to be followed if contact was lost. On the 9th November, Bennett signalled to Gander that he was arriving in a Hudson and that all aircraft were to be prepared for an immediate departure.

A crew member wrote, "He arrived himself on the seventh plane which completed the flight and within half an hour we knew we were to go that same night. When we gathered for briefing in the Control Tower we realised the enormous knowledge of aviation that this man had. In the few hours he had been there he had studied the weather maps and the forecasts and made out flight plans for each crew. Cruising cards had already been prepared, based upon the hours which he had spent on fuel consumption tests, radio facilities were at his finger tips. In fact there was not a question asked, so thoroughly had he covered every phase of this first flight."

In fact, it was impossible for Bennett to lead the formation that night; all the aircraft were heavily iced up. The top surfaces of the wings and the fuselage and the tailplane were coated with half an inch of clear steel-like ice that took a great deal of removing, and departure had to be postponed for twenty-four hours. Three hours after sunset on 10th November, 1940, he took off in reasonably good weather, each of the other aircraft following him in quick succession. The good people of Gander celebrated the

Lockheed Hudsons that were ferried in formation to the British Isles in the autumn of 1940.
RCAF Archives

event with a band, warmly wrapped against the cold, which standing in snow played "There'll always be an England." Each aircraft carried a captain, a second pilot and a wireless operator whose instructions were to keep a listening watch but not to break silence except in emergency. They carried rations provided by the railway car, sandwiches and coffee.

Bennett had estimated that the forecast twenty-three-knot tail wind component would enable the aircraft to reach Aldergrove in nine and a half hours. After take off, he handed over the controls to his American co-pilot and attended to the navigation, very much aware that with virtually no radio aids available he and his sextant were rather vital to the proceedings. As he put it, "The sense of heavy responsibility was somewhat peculiarly relieved by the knowledge that on this occasion at least one was appreciated." They flew at 16,000 feet but after a few hours the formation encountered a front. Bennett tried to climb above it, but this proved impossible

The inscription of the ferry command movement at Gander.

and he had to give the signal to separate. He knew that they were on track but he became worried about the severity of the icing and hoped that the others would be able to come to terms with it.

The Hudsons inevitably lost sight of one another. In addition to the problem of icing, the lack of oxygen bothered some of the crews; each aircraft had oxygen bottles but the supply was sufficient for only twenty minutes. Combined with the extreme cold, the effect on some was to induce a dreamy haze; a few temporarily lost consciousness. Bennett's order to maintain wireless silence was broken when one crew became alarmed as both engines cut. This had happened when a fuel tank ran dry before they had switched over to another tank, temporarily disturbing the forgetful pilots.

Bennett himself had no further problems and reached the coast of Ireland soon after daybreak, finding good visibility beneath the cloud. He arrived in the circuit at Aldergrove at the same time as another Hudson, and before long five of the seven were safely on the ground. Bennett went to the window of the control tower and waited. A crew member recalled that, "Bennett would not leave the window until the last plane was in and I have often wondered what his thoughts were as that seventh ship rolled to a stop. He had spent months of figuring and hours of hard work and finally himself led that first group to pioneer and prove it was possible to fly the North Atlantic in winter." Later, twenty two unshaven men—nine Americans, six British, six Canadians and one Australian—tried to convince the receptionist at a Belfast Hotel that they had just arrived from England. It was a necessary security measure, but the ten gallon hats, the high heeled Texan boots and the Canadian hooded parkas, led by Bennett's black Homburg hat and brief case, caused many penetrating looks.

To their intense annoyance, the crews were put on a ship for Canada that same day, unable to take back any personal impressions of England other than an air raid warning on the night they sailed from Liverpool. Bennett travelled to London to report personally to Beaverbrook. He had hoped to persuade the Minister that future flights would have to incorporate competent navigators and that good fortune had attended the inaugural formation flight, but the very success of the operation made it impossible to prove his argument. If fewer aircraft were lost than by sea, when the time between factory and delivery to the RAF took up to four months, Beaverbrook was well content.

The second formation flight across the Atlantic was led by Page, who was himself making the ocean crossing for the first time; Gordon Store was in charge on the third occasion. These three flights were all successful but winter conditions were obviously far too severe to make formation flying practicable. Bennett led the fourth formation himself in December, 1940, flying a Hudson that was a free gift to Britain, paid for by the aircraft workers of Lockheed and Vega. One aircraft swung on take-off and crashed, while a second had to fly back to Gander with technical trouble. Bennett returned to London and persuaded Beaverbrook to allow him to use RAF navigators who had completed their training in Canada. This was agreed, and when Bennett reached Montreal the first batch had already arrived to be given further instruction. Undoubtedly they learnt more about astro-navigation from Bennett than throughout their entire training. Whereas the pilots and wireless operators remained with the organisation, the RAF navigators were intended to make the one delivery flight, and the sector between Montreal served as part of their training. Despite their very limited experience the system proved successful and was continued.

Early in 1941, Bennett received a signal from the Air Ministry asking him to visit the Directorate of Bomber Operations on his next visit to England. His status since he had left the RAF in 1935

Atlantic ferry crews at Gander in late winter, 1940. Captain Gordon Store (in civilian clothes, third from the left) led one of the Hudson formation flights to the UK.

was that of civilian but in the face of a major problem that was troubling Bomber Command one of his former colleagues still in the service recalled that he was an expert navigator. The surrender of France and the Battle of Britain which had followed had enabled the RAF to abandon the futile practice of dropping leaflets over Germany in favour of a retaliatory campaign of bombing. However, photo reconnaissance of targets subsequent to Bomber Command's raids revealed no sign of damage and it had reluctantly been accepted that the crews had not dropped their bombs anywhere near the intended places; occasionally the area bombed was as much as eighty miles away. Bennett had been invited to express his views as a navigator.

He reminded them that the navigators had not had any practical experience of genuine operational flying, having been trained in distant and peaceful parts of the world. "Could you", he asked, "get into an aircraft on a pitch black night, fly for three or four hours on a compass and an airspeed indicator, avoid spoofs and dummies, not be put off by night fighters, flak and searchlights and guarantee success?" He pointed out that it required a force of experienced navigators to lead the crews, having first been provided with something better than the usual equipment. They would also have to be furnished with a distinctive type of fireworks to attract the main force to the target; the chances of success would thus be greatly improved. "It was the first seed", he wrote, "that I sowed on the subject of the Pathfinder Force which was subsequently to turn Bomber Command from failure to success." At the time Bennett had no idea that he would be returning to the RAF or that he would himself be appointed to put his own ideas into practice.

Bennett was back in North America when he was informed that a Hudson was missing on its way to Gander. The RCAF had taken charge of the search operation and decided not to permit the Hudsons already assembled at Gander to participate. Bennett signalled Gander that he would be arriving early next day and that the Hudsons were to be prepared for the search. The ferry pilots had been angered by the earlier decision and when Bennett landed he found that some of them had already taken off to look for their missing colleagues. He was still at the airport when one of these pilots reported that he had spotted the crashed machine and was circling the spot. Bennett got together some blankets and bundles of supplies and took off. He found the Hudson on the edge of a frozen lake partly concealed by trees. The pilot was visible and so was the message he had marked on the snow, "Three dead." The bundles were dropped and seen to be collected, and Bennett had just started back to Gander to organise a relief expedition when he spotted two men with a dog and sledge on another lake close by.

Messages wrapped in packages were dropped to them and the aircraft flown over their heads in the direction of the wreck. Returning to Gander, Bennett secured the assistance of the pilot of a DH Moth fitted with skis, but when they landed on the lake there was no sign of the survivor, as he had already been rescued by the sledge men. The three dead included a passenger, Dr Banting, celebrated for his development of insulin in the treatment of diabetes. It was established that engine failure on a fully laden aircraft which had partially iced up had caused the crash.

During that first winter there had been a change in the administration and Woods Humphery had resigned, to be replaced by a Canadian with no experience of any major airline operation nor of the Atlantic. However he was in Bennett's own words "an honest bush pilot with common sense who knew his limitations and would let me get on with my part of the job without any interference." This worked perfectly, but the success of the Atlantic Ferry had caused it to become a political football and there were some who wanted to take it away from Canadian Pacific. Acting on behalf of Beaverbrook, Morris Wilson appointed over everybody a man associated with the steel industry, Harold Long. "He was extremely fat, extremely soft," Bennett wrote, "and wore thick lensed glasses which apparently were not sufficiently effective to prevent him from finding his range from his associates until he had walked up to them so closely that his tummy touched them. In my opinion he was a dead loss in every way . . . as far as I was concerned I had never known such a catastrophe at any stage of my career. However we managed to get along in spite of him."

Lord Beaverbrook, Minister for Aircraft Production, 1940, who sent Captain Bennett to organize the Atlantic Ferry.
Express Newpapers

Powell's impression of this appointment was somewhat different. "Mr Long worked hard on a no-remuneration basis, a dollar-a-year man. He was not versed at all in aviation matters but he was a good business manager and it was evident to him from an early date that whereas Captain Wilcockson was supposed to be in control of operations, everything was in fact decided and acted upon by Captain Bennett. Technically Don Bennett was superb, but in terms of management style Harold Long and he were poles apart . . . Mr Long said that he and his colleagues simply could not get on with him."

The number of aircraft being delivered and successfully flown across the Atlantic increased. Bennett knew that the RCAF was keen to take over the organisation, and as President Roosevelt was keen to give Britain all possible assistance short of bringing the USA into the war, so the USAF became interested also. The arrival of Air Chief Marshal Dowding on an inspection confirmed Bennett's suspicions that changes were intended. He flew Dowding back to England on the first of the organisation's Return Ferry services, made possible by the delivery of some B-24 Liberators.

The runway at Montreal had a surface of bitumen, but the thaw which had followed the winter weather meant that there was virtually a river flowing a foot or so beneath it and there was therefore a danger involved in taking off a heavy four engined aircraft. Bennett's solution was to have wooden strips built on one end of the runway extending a sufficient distance for the aircraft to get rolling. The aircraft was towed out without fuel or load on to the wooden area, where it was refuelled. "I was disturbed", Bennett admitted, "at the way the tarmac rippled ahead of the aircraft wheels like an ocean swell crossed with a piece of sponge cake." He was very relieved when his plan worked and he was able to get the Liberator airborne without the wheels first penetrating the runway surface.

Another problem arose as Bennett prepared to land at Gander; the undercarriage handle was operated but the nose wheel jammed on its doors and would not extend. Bennett handed over the controls to the co-pilot and lowered himself into the nose to try to hold the doors clear as the handle was repeatedly operated. Eventually Bennett succeeded in lowering the nose wheel, at the expense of two fingers severely gashed.

On the eastbound journey to the British Isles, cargo was carried in the Liberators and so were "Very Important Passengers". Not for them the comforts and cosseting of present day travellers in the first class compartment of a long distance jet; they had to be content with mattresses laid in the bomb bay. Bennett believed that his return trip to Canada was the first direct landplane flight from the British Isles to Montreal; it took a few minutes under seventeen hours. The Return Ferry Service eliminated the sea journeys of three weeks or more which the pilots and wireless operators had previously had to endure after each delivery flight.

To release the British pilots for more urgent duties, the USAF took over responsibility for the delivery of aircraft as far as Montreal and Air Chief Marshal Bowhill arrived from England to replace Bennett. Beaverbrook had been removed from the Ministry of Aircraft Production, "given the push", Bennett thought, "because he was unpopular with senior RAF officers." This was an understatement; Beaverbrook had certainly been determined to break through the entrenched conventions of the Air Ministry and the long term plans of those to whom he always referred as "the bloody Air Marshals".

The main point of difference between Beaverbrook and the Air Ministry was the conviction of the former that strategic bombing could not by itself win the war. He was enthusiastic about fighter production whilst the air marshals were demanding priority in the manufacture of heavy bombers. Beaverbrook upset them when he increased the supply of aircraft to the Fleet Air Arm, and when the army commanders in the Middle East pleaded for dive bombers to give support to their ground troops he showed his sympathy by ordering a number from North America. The response of the Air Ministry was to refuse to supply or to train pilots to man these aircraft. Finally, Beaverbrook's willingness to accede to the proposal of the Admiralty's Sea Lords that the RAF Coastal Command should be placed under their own operational control drew furious protests form Lord Trenchard and the air marshals.

It struck Bennett as ironic that his own job should go to Bowhill, because the latter had vigorously opposed the creation of the Atlantic Ferry Organisation, insisting that it would be suicide to fly across the North Atlantic in winter. "I do not hold it against those who were of that opinion," he wrote. "At that time they knew no better." Upon his arrival, Air Chief Marshal Bowhill told Bennett that there was no longer any room for him and that as he had never been able to work alongside Harold Long it would be better if he went. He did so, flying home as pilot of a Hudson on a routine delivery flight. Of his exodus Powell wrote, "An accustomed technical thruster departed from the scene."

After her husband's appointment to the Atlantic Ferry Organisation Ly Bennett and her two children had travelled by sea to Canada, and Bowhill now gave his permission for them to fly back to England on one of the Boeing flying boats which had just been acquired by BOAC and put on the Atlantic service. Three such flying boats had been ordered by the Under Secretary of State for Air, Balfour, without obtaining the consent of Beaverbrook or the War Cabinet. The former had been furious at the minister's action, quite unprepared to concede to his colleague the right to adopt the independent initiatives which he had so freely practised himself. The Bennett children were probably the youngest passengers to have flown the Atlantic up to that time.

Back in London, Bennett called on Beaverbrook at his Ministry's office, which the latter was on the point of leaving. He congratulated the airman on the good work he had done and remarked that he was himself about to go to Canada, travelling by the Return Ferry Service. Bennett warned him to make sure that he was accommodated on that Liberator of the two then in Prestwick whose heater could be expected to function, as the other would first roast him and then cease to provide any heat at all. Beaverbrook took this advice and insisted on changing from the aircraft assigned to him. It was as well for him that he did; the other one crashed, killing all on board.

Many years later, Bennett's work for the Atlantic Ferry received its deserved acknowledgement. In 1967, when Canada was celebrating the centenary of the constitution of the Dominion with an exhibition in Montreal, he and his wife were invited to be the official guests of the Newfoundland Government on a visit to the exhibition and thereafter to Newfoundland. The invitation was accepted and in due course they flew up to Gander on a day chosen by the authorities. Bennett knew that some sort of ceremony was planned but he received surprise when the official car drew up before an RCAF guard of honour and, to record for future generations his own part in the history of Gander, a Hudson mounted on a plinth bearing the name *Spirit of Lockheed and Vega*.

* * *

Air Vice Marshal Bennett lays a wreath at the memorial commemorating RAF Ferry Command.
Bennett family

Attack on the Tirpitz   4

WHEN BOWHILL replaced Bennett in Montreal he told him he would be allowed to rejoin the RAF with the rank of acting group captain. Whilst awaiting a posting he again made contact with the Directorate of Bomber Operations. On this occasion he learnt that the ideas he had suggested for a target finding force to lead the bomber crews had been turned down and that for the time being there was little to be done. It was suggested to Bennett that he should try to join a bomber squadron and continue to press his ideas.

Six weeks were spent in frustrating idleness while junior civil servants declared that it was impossible to offer an apparent civilian a senior position in uniform. Finally, when Bennett was offered a job as a squadron leader, he admitted, "I really became annoyed at that, told them what I thought of it, with the result that I was up-graded one notch and sent to Eastbourne as an acting wing commander to be second in command of a new elementary air navigation school."

To the extent that it was a new scheme and 2,000 navigators would receive their initial training there, the job was important, but it did not require anyone with the knowledge of advanced navigation that Bennett possessed. In fact, the duties assigned to him were mainly administrative, organising the school itself, the syllabus, the layout of classrooms and even the accommodation of the cadets in commandeered hotels within Eastbourne. His relations with his commanding officer were less than happy and he recalled that the latter at their first meeting "appeared pompous and icy . . . I had to exercise considerable self control."

Bennett stayed long enough to get the first class started and then informed his CO that he believed that he would be more use in Bomber Command. "He was very decent about it," he remembered, "and even gave me the tip to see . . . the personnel officer at Bomber Command who would surely welcome somebody with a lot of flying experience." This officer did indeed welcome him with open arms. "I was a squadron commander on the spot and had hardly time to get my breath before I found myself in Yorkshire, cold and miserable, but delighted at last to be taking part in the shooting war."

77 Squadron at Leeming was equipped with Armstrong Whitworth Whitleys and operated within 4 Group, which was commanded by Air Vice Marshal Roderic Carr. Bennett was

*Air Vice Marshal Sir
Roderic Carr, who
commanded 4 Group
Bomber Command and
invariably supported
Bennett's initiatives.*
Mr Martin Carr

delighted to renew his acquaintance with Carr, who had been very helpful to Atlantic Ferry when he had earlier held a command in Northern Ireland. It was a disappointment that the squadron had not yet been supplied with four engined bombers, but the obsolescent Whitleys were still delivering half the bombs then being dropped on Germany.

On his arrival at Leeming Bennett reported to the station commander. At once a flash of recognition and recollection passed between the two officers. Bennett remembered that Bill Staton was "a worthy group captain with whom I had had to be rather firm in Montreal" and who had arrived with some junior RAF officers to make one trip for the Ferry Organisation. "He had apparently felt it beneath his dignity to associate with civilians . . . ignored a number of administrative requirements of the Atlantic Ferry and I had therefore to ask him to report to my office. He came to my office in the centre of Montreal in shorts. Without much ado I told him to get out and come back properly dressed. He was a little troublesome and eventually I had to make it quite clear that either he complied with our requirements or I would put him straight back on a ship for England."

It was clear to Bennett that his commanding officer had not forgotten their previous meeting. His welcoming speech could be summed up as "I am the only cock that crows on this muck heap . . . you remember that." Bennett assured Staton that he was fully aware of the need for discipline in the Royal Air Force and would cause no trouble. "I must say," he wrote, "I was a little glad when in a very short period after my arrival at Leeming he was posted overseas." The two men were not to meet again until 1960 when Staton was the plaintiff, Bennett the defendant charged with libel.

Staton issued one order to Bennett which the latter accepted as thoroughly sensible. This was that he should fly as second pilot on two flights over enemy territory before he flew a bomber in command. He chose the two most inexperienced sergeant pilots in the Squadron and flew with each in turn. On the second trip, when the pilot was preoccupied with anti-aircraft fire, Bennett noticed that the oil pressure gauge of one engine was winding down and correctly guessed that it was the instrument and not the engine which was unserviceable. The pilot disregarded this diagnosis of the problem, shut down the engine and pressed on to the target with the power available from the other engine. As a straggler from the main force the aircraft attracted an immense amount of flak, but when the bomb aimer, blinded by the searchlights, called for a second run over the target and then a third, without having released the bombs, Bennett decided to assume command himself. The Whitley had already drifted from 14,000 feet down to 8,000 feet and was becoming an increasingly easy target for the guns. He dropped the bomb load, restarted the engine, flew out of the target area and then handed over the controls to the sergeant pilot.

The lesson he had learned was that bomber operations were entrusted to young men with very little technical knowledge or experience but, in his own words, "the courage of a thousand lions". After these two trips Bennett flew with a different crew on each night's operations, replacing their usual captain. His object was to find out how well each crew member performed his particular job and also to pass on to them his own very considerable navigational knowledge.

In 1937, the Air Ministry had been informed by the C in C, Bomber Command, that the rapid expansion of the RAF was proceeding without sufficient training being given to the new recruits who would man the aircraft. Particularly he had in mind the navigators, then known as air observers. Even in 1938, their training amounted to only a ten week course and they were expected to perform other duties besides navigation; very often they were accorded only non-commissioned rank. The inevitable result was that when the war started, half the navigators could not even find a "target" in a friendly city in daylight and in good weather. Their difficulties were multiplied by the inaccuracies of the primitive compasses and airspeed indicators in use, the need to depend upon assumed wind strength and direction, alterations of course by the pilot to avoid flak or fighters and long periods in cloud. Only a skilled navigator could use a sextant to establish his position, and when this was plotted on his chart it recorded where the aircraft had been twenty minutes earlier.

Accuracy of navigation was an urgent priority. Precision was poor and the crews had never been taught how to "swing" a compass in the air. Night photography from bomber aircraft to establish what results were being obtained from each Whitley's bomb load was rarely practised. Bennett's efforts to obtain better results were rewarded when he insisted upon his crews returning from operations with photographs, and he demanded an explanation from those who failed to do so.

As far as could be ascertained at squadron level there seemed to be no particular policy in regard to targets. Sometimes north German ports or industrial targets inland were attacked and then easy targets in occupied France would be chosen. Most of Bomber Command attacked the lightly defended Renault works in the Paris area one afternoon, and when Bennett made his run in at 2,000 feet the bomb bursts below severely rocked his aircraft. Over another target in the Paris area his bomb aimer had such poor night vision that well over an hour and a half was spent trying to find the aiming point; during this period a German night fighter was trying to get on his tail so that he was forced to make tight turns. Upon his return to Leeming he found about fifty holes in the Whitley and one of the flying control cables had been hit and almost severed.

77 Squadron taught Bennett some interesting lessons concerning the thoughts and beliefs of young men who on first acquaintance might appear to be shallow. A Canadian pilot asked for a private interview. He was greatly disturbed to have been ordered to bomb what he regarded as a civilian target and he declared himself unable to do such a thing, as he was only prepared to make war against the armed forces of the enemy. Bennett tried to explain that in modern conditions of warfare the entire population of Germany was engaged in the fight, if not in uniform, then in armaments factories and the like. "I think I helped him," he wrote, "but there was no doubt that for a long period his conscience worried him whenever there was any target which was not glaringly military in character."

The casualty rate at that time was about five per cent each raid, and with each crew being expected to take part in thirty raids before being temporarily assigned to more peaceful duties, the chances of survival were not high. Many aircraft crashed on their return to Leeming, either as a result of damage caused by gunfire during the raid or by errors on the part of pilots suffering the combined efforts of strain and fatigue. It was particularly galling to Bennett that when he reached the scene of the crash on such occasions he arrived there considerably sooner than the airfield fire fighting services. One Whitley crashed half a mile short of the runway and beyond the river Swale, the fuel tanks burst and a sheet of flame eighty feet high suddenly erupted. By then Bennett had waded across the river and extracted one of the crew, but sadly this man died two days later.

Bennett's increasing conviction that the war was not being pursued with anything like an adequate sense of initiative and energy was reinforced when the German warships *Scharnhorst* and *Gneisenau*, which had been in harbour in Brest, were observed by a patrolling fighter pilot to be heading for the English Channel. They were steaming in good weather with an escort of smaller vessels and protected by a fighter screen overhead. These aircraft were clearly visible on British radar displays on the south coast and Bennett learned of this on a visit to the operations room. 10 Squadron, which had been re-equipped with Halifaxes, had been called to readiness but his own had not, and his request to have 77 Squadron involved was turned down. His further insistence was rewarded by permission to have his squadron brought to readiness and to await further orders. All day and into the evening the crews stood by without being called.

German battle cruiser Gneisenau *in Brest harbour dry dock. Photograph by Spitfire pilot P/O Chandler, 1941.* RAF Museum

Bennett wrote, "Instead of choosing the moment when the maximum possible effective forces could be formed together and then flung into the attack with all possible speed, the idea of an attack on two warships was to play at it with penny numbers frittered away little by little. There was no cohesion, no co-ordination and never at any time was there any effective strength deployed against these ships." In fact, six Swordfish biplanes of the Fleet Air Arm were ordered to attempt a torpedo attack on the German vessels. It is hard to quarrel with Bennett's opinion that "it was one of the most suicidal operations I have ever known." All of the Swordfish were shot down. They were led by a former Imperial Airways captain, Eugene Esmond, who was awarded a posthumous Victoria Cross. Some Beaufort torpedo aircraft also failed to prevent the warships reaching their destination.

Bennett had shared the opinion of many RAF officers that the bomber offensive against Germany provided the only means of victory. There seemed in 1942 insurmountable problems in establishing a foothold back in Europe unless the military might of the enemy, backed by their huge industrial capacity, could be destroyed. Yet the bomber offensive such as it was had so far not been effective. Bennett was not slow to realise that the majority of the crews were not finding the target area at all, whilst those who did failed to identify the aiming point. In many cases they did not

*Handley Page Halifax of
10 Squadron*

bother to aim. There was a general impression that one could not miss a large German city so it did not matter whether the bombs hit a particular target within it. It was more evident than ever that a target-finding force was necessary and it was also encouraging to know that senior officers of the Directorate of Bomber Operations shared his view that Bomber Command's offensive had been wasteful and largely ineffective. Bennett was greatly cheered when it became known that his original squadron commander at Pembroke Dock, now Air Chief Marshal Sir Arthur Harris, had been appointed Commander in Chief of Bomber Command.

In April, 1942, Bennett was transferred from 77 Squadron to the Command of 10 Squadron which was also at Leeming and was equipped with Halifax bombers. One night his squadron was assigned to a target requested by the Royal Navy, the *Tirpitz*, which was in Aasfjord near Trondheim, Norway. It was lying close inshore and the Admiralty wanted some spherical mines to be dropped on to the sloping banks of the fjord. This was to be achieved at night and at low level, so a clear moonlit night was chosen. Naval intelligence reported that the selected track for the run-in was free from defences. In addition to 10 Squadron another Halifax squadron was also detailed and every aircraft was loaded with five mines, each weighing 1,000 lbs. As they crossed the Norwegian coast they encountered considerable anti-aircraft fire, and as the *Tirpitz* was approached all the units of the German fleet in the fjord opened up, whilst a man-made mist suddenly covered the target area. Bennett's aircraft was repeatedly hit, his tail gunner wounded. The starboard wing began to burn fiercely, the starboard wheel came down and the flap began to trail. He released the mines and turned east towards Sweden, opening up the engines in an attempt to climb, but the aircraft wing was still blazing and it became obvious that the Halifax could not possibly be flown above the mountains, which rose steeply to about three thousand feet a little to the east of the target area. Bennett told the flight engineer to help the wounded air gunner to bail out, then he gave the order, "Abandon aircraft, jump, jump!" Only after giving this order, sitting alone and trying to hold the wings level by aileron and full port rudder, did he remember that he was not wearing his parachute, the type which had to be clipped on to the harness over the pilot's chest. The flight engineer, to Bennett's immense surprise and relief, suddenly reappeared and risked his own life by finding the parachute in the fuselage and attaching it to his pilot's harness. By this time the aircraft was losing height rapidly and the ground was very close, and as Bennett left his seat the burning starboard wing crumpled up. He jumped through the open hatch and pulled the ripcord as soon as he was clear; his parachute opened just as he was about to strike the snow, but he picked himself up uninjured.

He gathered in the parachute, rolled it round the harness and covered it with snow. He was in fairly open country with few trees and he made it his first task to put as large a distance as possible between himself and the crashed Halifax, heading in an easterly direction. Occasionally he heard voices and this spurred his efforts; after about an hour he encountered a very fast-running stream between steep banks coated with ice. He had entered a wooded area; it was almost daylight but the trees made it appear dark. Bennett was trying to find a way of getting across the stream when he found himself face to face with a man. His first thought was that this was a German but the man raised his hands above his head and only then did he recognise his wireless operator. Together they went on, but the stream presented a problem until it was established, by the use of a pole found among the trees, that it was not so deep that its violence would prevent a crossing. They waded across and emerged on much higher ground bare of trees but covered with snow and rocks. The combination of sun and snow affected their vision, and in their exhausted state they imagined that they could see houses. Both had their escape kits in their pockets and in addition to some Horlicks tablets and barley sugar these contained a silk handkerchief on which was printed a map of the area. Small in scale as it was, the map proved invaluable. There was also a small rubber bag which they could fill with water or failing that snow, which melted in the warmth of their pockets.

If they were going to survive, they had to take the risk of meeting Germans. The map showed a railway line to the north and by late afternoon they reached it and walked along the line until they came upon a railway station. There seemed to be no sign of life but closer inspection revealed an unsuspecting railway official

55

reading beneath a light in his office. They hoped to continue along the railway line, so much easier going than the snow, but suddenly they came upon a railway bridge across a river, on the near side of which a sentry box appeared to contain a man. In their weakened state it seemed too great a risk to try to overpower him so they retreated and made their way up a slope near the river, where at almost midnight they came upon a small house with a light in the doorway. Cold and miserable, they knocked on the door, but there was no answer so they entered and called again. The clothing on the hooks in the hall did not look like German military wear, and undecided what to do they went outside and noticed a shed. Investigation revealed a heavy fur sleigh rug, under which they lay down and instantly fell asleep. Within an hour, however, the intense cold woke them up and they decided to resume the journey to the mountains. It had been −15°C according to a thermometer in the house, and as they walked the temperature seemed to get even colder. Late in the afternoon of that second day they saw another house and when they knocked on the door it was opened by a little girl who looked in terror at the two strangers and ran back indoors. A man and a woman appeared and stared. Bennett asked them in English for food, pointing at his mouth, rubbing his stomach, accepting that they would not understand what he was saying. They continued to stare, showing no sign of friendship, so without taking his eye off the couple he said to his companion, "Get ready to run, run as fast as you can when I give you the word to go."

There was an immediate reaction. The man grinned and in perfect English said, "It's quite all right. Come in." Apparently the police had been looking for British airmen and he was worried that this might be a German ruse to try to trick him. At last the two airmen were able to lie down in warm conditions for a proper sleep, but Bennett got a shock when he was woken to find himself staring into the faces of two strangers. Fear that they might be Germans turned to relief when he learnt that these were the Norwegians who were to lead them in the direction of safety. Before they would leave, positive proof of identification was demanded and Bennett handed over the watch given to him by Sperry's, the American gyro manufacturers, on the occasion of his seaplane record in 1938. This bore his name.

First one and then another Norwegian escorted them towards the Swedish border. The second of these pointed to some distant ridge five miles further on. "Sweden," he said. There they observed stone hummocks on opposite sides of which different colours denoted the frontier. They hurried on, fearful that a German patrol might not hesitate to pursue them across an uninhabited expanse of snow and grateful as night fell to see lights in the distance. They reached a building through whose uncurtained windows couples could be seen dancing. They knocked on the back door and once again a young girl opened it, stared in alarm and slammed the door in their faces. But two men joined them, greeting them in perfect English, "Welcome to Sweden, come inside." There was a great commotion, the dancers swarming round to shake them by the hand.

After a generous dinner, a courteous Swedish army captain formally put them under arrest, escorted them to a comfortable bedroom and locked the door from the outside. The next day, before a Swedish air force officer took them by train into internment in central Sweden, Bennett persuaded the army captain to send a cable to Ly Bennett with the single word "Love". Bennett and his wife had used this method of communication throughout the years to confirm a safe arrival and he knew that she would immediately realise its significance. She reported the arrival of the cable to the station commander at Leeming and he rushed over to the cottage near the airfield where she was living. Together they found in an atlas the Swedish town from which the cable had been sent. The Air Ministry was informed and a few days later Ly Bennett was officially notified that "From an unreliable source we are advised that Wing Commander Bennett is alive and in Sweden."

In the internment camp, a collection of cold wooden huts, Bennett was delighted to find his second pilot and flight engineer. Only later did he learn that the other three members of his crew including the wounded air gunner had survived and were prisoners of war of the Germans. Meanwhile, as he and the other internees were allowed to visit the local town, Bennett lost no time in telephoning the British Legation in Stockholm. He pointed out that having avoided capture as prisoners of war they did not have belligerent status so should not be interned. He was considerably irked to be informed that the Swedish authorities might not take the same viewpoint. In fact, it was a Swedish friend who suggested that he apply for parole to go to Stockholm and put his case himself. The Swede had an Australian wife; they had read in the Stockholm newspapers that an Australian pilot had escaped to their country from Norway and they had made the journey to the internment camp to visit him.

The British Minister and Air Attaché were kind and courteous but Bennett considered them "far too mild for my liking. If I had left it to them I should have been interned for anything up to a year." It was his Swedish friend once again who arranged a meeting with Count Bernadotte of the Swedish Foreign Office. Progress was made; he was allowed to remain in Stockholm and in due course his release was agreed. During that time Bennett discussed the raid on the *Tirpitz* with the British Naval Attaché, who showed him the reports on the German defences along the Norwegian coast which prior to the raid he had sent to London. It was particularly infuriating to Bennett that this information had never been passed to the Halifax squadrons. If this had been done he was sure that it would have been possible to plan a more successful form of attack. Subsequent enquiries brought from the Admiralty the response that such information was purely for naval purposes, and this did nothing to improve Bennett's opinion of the senior service.

The return to England was in a Lockheed 14 which regularly ran the gauntlet through the Kattegat in the hours of darkness. On this occasion the aircraft's pilot was given a forecast showing so much cloud that he decided to leave in daylight, and to Bennett's horror the most dangerous area was flown in almost perfectly clear weather. "That we should get through," he wrote, "simply proves the magnificent value of surprise. No stupid German could have imagined that any stupid Englishman could be so stupid as to do a thing such as that. So we survived." The Lockheed landed at Leuchars, from where Bennett had a few years before set off in *Mercury* for his record-breaking flight to South Africa. The pilot of an Anson flew him down to Leeming for a reunion with Ly and the children, whom he had last seen one month earlier.

There was a formality to be attended to in London, however. The Air Ministry Intelligence Department wanted to ensure that he had not killed any Germans in the process of escaping, for if he had done so Bennett would not have been permitted to fly over enemy territory again. He was able to reassure the department on this point and was allowed to resume command of his squadron. This visit to London meant that he was unable to take part in the first thousand bomber raid that the C in C had mounted against Cologne. This was a great disappointment, as it was the most successful of the three that were staged at that time. He had however renewed his acquaintance with Air Chief Marshal Harris, who informed him that he had been granted an immediate award of the Distinguished Service Order.

During that summer of 1942, 10 Squadron was ordered to the Middle East to take part in operations against the Italian fleet. This was not a welcome assignment to Bennett, whose combative spirit saw Germany as the main enemy and the Italians as very little threat to the Allies in any way. The squadron had already moved south to Hurn when within an hour or so of their departure time a signal arrived ordering him to hand over command to one of the flight commanders and to report once again to the Commander-in-Chief, Bomber Command. He was about to learn that his hopes were to be realised; the Pathfinder Force was to be created.

The Formation of Pathfinder Force   5

HARRIS HAD been fighting a rearguard action in opposition to the concept of a target finding force. It was his view that "area bombing" of enemy cities would eventually so demoralise the Germans and disrupt their industrial capacity that in the end the war could be won without the need to land troops in Europe. Harris had been impressed by the fact that the "Blitz" on London had resulted in a greater loss of man-hours than damage to factories. He looked upon the Ruhr valley as the most fruitful area for bombing because the German economy depended so much upon industry there.

Harris foresaw, rightly as it turned out, that there would be ill feeling among the groups in his Command if they were ordered to release their best crews to be incorporated into a corps d'élite. He had suggested that the target-finding task should be allocated to whichever squadron had produced the best photographs during the raids of the preceding month; alternatively each group could form its own target finding squadron. In the early part of the war he had himself been Deputy Chief of Air Staff and had regarded the staff officers of the "fantastically bloated" departments with unconcealed contempt. Consequently, Harris had resented and resisted pressure from the Directorate of Bomber Operations under its Director, Group Captain Bufton, for the creation of a specialised target-finding force. Bufton regarded area bombing as a transitory phase after which smaller, primarily strategic, targets would have to be located by improved ground and airborne equipment and systematically destroyed. Ultimately, Harris had received a direct order from the Chief of Air Staff, Air Chief Marshal Portal, to bring the new Force into being.

Harris had summoned Bennett to inform him that he was to be put in command of the corps d'élite but he made no secret of the fact that he had done his best to prevent its formation. Nor would he allow it to be called the Target-Finding Force because, Bennett surmised, that title had been chosen by the Directorate. He would call it the Pathfinder Force. Bennett would be promoted to groupcaptain and allocated a headquarters to manage the Pathfinders. He would be free to select a suitable station for this purpose and other aerodromes conveniently close to it. Harris

Air Chief Marshal Harris, Bomber Command, who chose Bennett to command the Pathfinders.
RAF Museum

promised Bennett that he would accord his personal support to the Pathfinder Force without wasting any efforts on it.

Inevitably Harris had run into further opposition from the Air Ministry when he chose a youthful wing commander with limited administrative experience to command the new organisation. Subsequently he was to write, "I had known Bennett since 1931 . . . he was the obvious man available for the job of head of Pathfinder Force. Still in his early thirties he was very young indeed to be a group commander but his technical knowledge and operational ability were altogether exceptional. His moral and physical courage was outstanding and he was an unrivalled technician." Harris also noted Bennett's unusually good memory and his ability to master in a very short time the intricacies of the most technical subjects. "He was the most efficient airman I have ever met."

Bennett observed that Harris had grown fatter than he had been in 1931 but gave the impression of youthfulness in his genial personality. Like many "coppernobs" his golden hair gave an indication of his short temper and outspoken style. He could be very rude indeed when expressing disapproval and he was not very popular with the most senior officers of the Royal Navy and the Army, who frequently incurred his anger. Bennett had been greatly encouraged when Harris had taken over at Bomber Command, expecting there to be a more intelligent and aggressive direction of effort against Germany. Both men were stubborn and combined that ingredient with the faculty of usually being right in their opinions. Neither had much time for diplomacy when they wanted to cut through red tape and obstruction and their criticism was usually expressed in blunt terms. Both therefore had relatively few friends among the senior officers with whom they had to work.

Harris told Bennett that for maximum effectiveness the crews of Pathfinder Force would be required to fly on fifty sorties against enemy targets before completing their tour of operations. This was more than the usual number of thirty raids, and for this reason there would be special recognition. There would be a step-up in rank and the right to wear a distinctive badge, the RAF eagle, below medal ribbons. As Harris had predicted, the goodwill shown towards Pathfinder Force was minimal, and for the most part group commanders were reluctant to encourage their crews to volunteer. Ground crews, aircraft and spares had also to be made available by other groups in the Command. A wrangle developed with the Treasury over the extra cost involved in wholesale promotions; this delayed the arrival of crews for six weeks. Bennett visited the group commanders and discovered for himself the scale of their resentment. Only Air Vice Marshal Carr willingly offered support, and those group commanders who prevented all their best crews from volunteering were not put under pressure from

Harris to be more co-operative. Many crews who did volunteer could not meet Bennett's high standards and were sent back to their former units. For Bennett the selection and training of crews was the most vital consideration. Those who were chosen had subsequently to earn the respect of others who were jealous.

Bennett had been authorised to select the stations where he wished his first squadrons to be based and made his choice on the basis of good communications and weather record. He made Wyton his headquarters and had the use of Oakington, Gravely and Worboys. The squadrons were equipped with Stirlings, Halifaxes, Lancasters and Wellingtons. There were in fact two squadrons equipped with the twin engined Wellington; the aircraft of one of these squadrons had been fitted with pressure chambers so that they could be flown at 30,000 feet. These enormous steel boilers so reduced the carrying capacity that Bennett was not keen to use them. In the course of a test flight he developed an infection in both ears when at 6,000 feet a crew member mistakingly took the cabin pressure to that for 30,000 feet in a second and then reversed the process over twenty or thirty seconds when he reacted over-hastily to his initial mistake. Bennett's decision not to use the pressurised Wellingtons was greeted with delight by those who were expected to fly in them.

As a squadron commander at Leeming he had taken the trouble to study the job of each crew member until he himself knew how it should be done. In his new role he addressed all recruits to the Pathfinder Force when they attended a two week course at Worboys before posting to a squadron. When he interviewed new crews they were always impressed by the very extensive knowledge he possessed; he did not tolerate mistakes and axed anyone who could not uphold the expected standards. He greatly appreciated of the initiative of Harris in identifying each member of a Pathfinder crew by the eagle badge but in other respects he demanded anonymity and refused to have a public relations officer or any publicity directed to the Force. He declared that there would be no professional heroes or stars and no living holders of the Victoria Cross among their number. One military historian was to write, "He made no secret of his opinion that his appointment represented the eclipse of the Gentlemen and the arrival of the Players."

In the period between July, 1942, when Bennett had been appointed, and the assembly of the first five Pathfinder squadrons he found the time to attend to the development and production of better forms of navigational equipment than had so far been available. During 1942, a device known as Gee had been introduced. It depended upon a "master" and two "slave" stations in England whose radar signals could be aligned and measured by

the navigator on his aircraft receiver. He could then speedily establish his position on the grid map with which he was provided. It had been hoped that this system would give sufficient accuracy in navigation to make blind bombing of the Ruhr practicable. Unfortunately, its accuracy decreased the further the aircraft was from the ground stations; Gee was not adequate for locating aiming points which were 300 miles from the English coast. The Germans also found ways of jamming it. However, Gee proved immensely valuable in assisting crews to return to their home stations, particularly in conditions of poor visibility.

More was expected of an airborne radar ground reflection system called H_2S, which it was hoped would be an excellent instrument for night navigation at any range from base in addition to serving as a target finding and blind-bombing device. The name has been attributed to Lord Cherwell, principal scientific adviser to Winston Churchill, who when asked for his comments was reported to have said, "It stinks. Call it H_2S." On their radar screens the bomber crews could differentiate between land and water and thus identify coast lines, estuaries and rivers; they could also pick out built-up areas when they were of appreciable size. The H_2S screen was provided with various range scales so that having reached the target area the bombing run could be made on the shortest scale. The foregoing represents the intention of the designers; some time was to elapse before serviceable radar sets were fitted in adequate quantity to bomber aircraft.

H_2S seemed to Bennett such a useful device, with such tremendous potential, that very soon after his appointment he visited the Telecommunication Research Establishment (TRE) at Great Malvern, situated close to the RAF station at Defford. A few days earlier the first aircraft to be fitted with a test rig for H_2S had crashed in the Welsh mountains with the loss of all on board. This served as a warning that H_2S did not recognise high ground, and thereafter a radio altimeter was incorporated to show the height of the aircraft above the land surface. One of the scientists ("boffins") in the H_2S team who met Bennett on his arrival was Dr (now Professor Sir) Bernard Lovell. The former was impatient to have the development programme accelerated and was exasperated by the apparent lack of urgency and pedantic approach of the TRE. As he put it, "They had the most old-fashioned pre-war RAF conception of maintenance and no idea whatever of getting on with the job. The fact that I required them to test-fly at all hours of the day and night shook them to the core." The equipment was being tested on Halifax aircraft, which were frequently unserviceable, so Bennett's solution was to ask Bomber Command for a detachment of competent mechanics accustomed to maintaining Halifaxes. He excluded Lovell and the boffins from his criticism and reported

Opposite page: *Air Commodore Bennett introduces his officers to Queen Elizabeth at RAF Wyton.* Bennett family

63

that they rallied round magnificently and put in a wonderful effort in getting H₂S into practical use so quickly. He acknowledged that H₂S with its eight boxes of complicated circuitry could have taken two years to develop but that within a month of his arrival fairly good results had been obtained during test flights.

In his diary Lovell wrote, "Bennett stood by at Defford most of July and caused considerable turmoil. He seemed to be happy only when flying at 5.30am or midnight." Nevertheless, the two men established an excellent working relationship and by July they were ready to put the case for using the system to Harris, who then had to persuade Churchill and Lord Cherwell. The reason for this was the employment within H₂S of a new invention called the magnetron, the secrets of which some Cabinet Ministers and other officials were fearful might be made available to the Germans when a bomber equipped with the system was shot down. Harris and Bennett had to fight hard to persuade the doubters that the advantages in achieving target identification far outweighed the dangers of disclosure of the secrets of the magnetron. Bennett paid a personal visit to Lord Cherwell to gain his support for using the equipment and eventually approval was given, but by the end of 1942 only fifty sets of H₂S had been produced.

During that summer Bennett was conducting discussions with the pyrotechnic experts with a view to the production of hooded flares, a device in the form of an umbrella above each one to prevent glareback in the eyes of the bomb aimer when he was trying to identify the target. Called target indicators, the flares were provided with a barometric fuse set to burst at a few hundred feet above the ground. They were manufactured in different colours and in combinations of colours, as the Germans had become very proficient in creating dummy target areas in open country, surrounded by searchlights and lit by their own incendiaries, to look like a real target to the bombers as they came upon the scene. Thus, given a specific colour for each raid, the Pathfinders could illuminate the target area with target indicators and the main force of the bomber squadrons were ordered to aim at them.

Anticipating the introduction of H₂S and the ability of navigators trained in its use to find targets completely obscured by cloud cover, Bennett also ordered the pyrotechnic experts to manufacture Sky Markers, parachute flares which could mark a spot above the cloud for the very limited period before the wind carried them away from the target. The sky markers were for use when the glow of target indicators bursting at low levels was obscured by cloud. Although ridiculed by some detractors as hopelessly inaccurate as aiming points, Bennett had no doubt that this method would be a considerable improvement on the slapdash bombing undertaken hitherto.

In August, 1942, the squadrons of the Pathfinder Force assembled. "Typical of the attitude of Bert Harris", wrote Bennett, "was the order which he issued to me to operate the day they arrived without missing a single night and that no period would be allowed for preparation or for training. This was quite unreasonable but the spirit behind it was so press-on that I made no attempt to argue." In fact bad weather resulted in all operations being cancelled that night, but twenty-four hours later the squadrons were ordered to attack Flensburg, a submarine base north of Kiel, using visual methods only, no radar devices being available. However, the clear weather forecast over the target area had given way to considerable low cloud; the chances of success were nil and the raid proved a complete failure, giving the cynics a chance to jeer at the Pathfinders.

Bennett set in train a programme of lectures and training in the air. Even using the old fashioned methods of ordinary navigation, results soon improved, thanks to the new target indicators. Losses of aircraft were also reduced by better tactical routing towards the targets, designed to lessen the dangers from heavily defended areas and to confuse the enemy as to the intended target.

Bennett was highly critical of a change of policy in crew complement which came into effect at the time Pathfinder Force began operations, when those at the Air Ministry responsible for air crew training decided that it was impossible to train enough pilots to carry two in every bomber. The large four engined aircraft being introduced included a flight engineer's panel and one pilot would have to suffice. It was Bennett's view that this weakened not only the strength of Bomber Command but the efficiency of Pathfinder Force. The policy of excluding a second pilot resulted in squadrons receiving new crews whose captains had never been tested under operational conditions, never seen a German target nor been shot at. Their inexperience made most of them relatively ineffective for much of their operational tour, whilst the loss rate during the first three trips of a new crew was five times as great as for the rest of the tour. This resulted in a loss of aircraft and effectiveness. Bennett would have preferred junior pilots to act as flight engineers on their first fifteen raids before being converted on to four engined aircraft, but he was unable to have the policy reversed. "This", he wrote, "was a typical example of maximum waste for minimum result. As with most policy decisions during the war it was taken by those who had never themselves operated under modern conditions."

One reason why Bennett had been keen to avoid the use of the pressurised Wellington was the availability of the small twin-engined de Havilland Mosquito. This machine had been developed

De Havilland Mosquito.
Ministry of Defence

as a private enterprise but the idea of an unarmed all-wooden-airframe bomber relying upon speed and manoeuvrability to evade fighters was not acceptable to the majority of the Air Council, and only one of their number, Sir Wilfred Freeman, had shown any enthusiasm for the design. Lord Beaverbrook, whilst Minister for Aircraft Production, had permitted production of an initial fifty because de Havilland had accepted his target date for completion and had not asked to be supplied with scarce materials.

Bennett had acquired a few of these unwanted Mosquitoes, as he was aware that the first twenty had performed very satisfactorily in a photo reconnaissance role. The bomb bay could accommodate an adequate number of target indicators and he satisfied himself in the course of a series of air tests that the aircraft could achieve the desired ceiling. There followed a meeting at the Air Ministry in the course of which the representatives of that ministry and Bomber Command both strongly opposed the adoption of the Mosquito. They argued that it was far too small to carry an adequate crew, too frail, too easy to shoot down because of the lack of gun turrets and incapable of carrying enough of a bomb load or equipment. Bennett dealt with each of these objections in turn but the opposition produced another reason for rejection: the Mosquito had been flight tested by the approved establishments and found to be almost impossible to fly at night. At this, he informed those present that he had been flying the aircraft regularly at night in the course of the past week and had found nothing wrong with it. This argument won him the Mosquitoes he wanted.

During the course of the early Pathfinder operations many lessons were learnt. The small number of Pathfinder aircraft which preceded the main force of bombers to the target attracted such a concentrated barrage from anti-aircraft guns that their job was made very difficult. To overcome this Bennett sent in "supporters" to divide the attention of the defences. There could not be too many of these however, because their heavy explosive bombs raised dust and smoke which could obscure the identification of the aiming point. They could not use incendiaries because glare made the task of the Pathfinder bomb aimers more difficult, whilst incendiaries dropped away from the correct target area undid the work of the markers. There was another constant problem: to send too few markers was to risk failure; to send too many was to expose the most valuable crews to excessive danger. Finally, the meteorological service available was unreliable, but pressure from Bennett was rewarded by having the meteorology flight put under his command.

The routine prior to each night's operations seldom varied. Bennett would go to his Operations Room together with his air staff and intelligence officers. A telephone message from Bomber Command HQ would notify him of the target and the number of aircraft to be deployed against it, while the Pathfinders' own meteorology officer would express his opinion as to the likely weather. Bennett and his immediate staff then decided upon the marking method and an alternative method in case the first choice proved not to be feasible. Next, the route to the target was chosen. Finally, the entire plan was passed through Bomber Command HQ to the groups providing the main force.

When the first thousand-bomber raid on Cologne had been undertaken prior to the formation of Pathfinder Force, one of its objects had been to observe the results of this attempt to saturate the defences. Air Vice Marshal Baldwin, commanding No. 3 Group, had flown in a bomber himself. The following day the Commander in Chief issued explicit instructions that no group commander should fly on operations without his permission, owing to the valuable operational knowledge in his possession which, if captured, he would be put under intense pressure to reveal. This was not the sort of order that a man of Bennett's temperament was inclined to obey. He had always made it a rule to attend the briefing at one of his stations prior to the night's operations and one interrogation when the crews returned. He also flew out to the targets himself on occasions to observe how effectively they were being marked. Furthermore, he required his own staff officers to operate at a reasonable frequency in order to ensure that they appreciated the whole concept of the Pathfinders' task.

In the first month of the Force's operations the staff officer responsible for navigation failed to return from a raid. It was on navigation above all else that good results depended and on two further occasions HQ staff navigation officers were to suffer the same fate. Both Bennett and those most critical of the Pathfinder idea were closely watching the losses of crews and aircraft, for there were some who believed that they would suffer the most grievous consequences and that the losses would be catastrophic. In August, 1942, their losses of 9 per cent of the aircraft deployed were rather worse than those of the main force. This figure did nothing to encourage further volunteers but a great improvement followed: 3 per cent in September and 2.6 per cent in October. Thereafter the losses never rose above 4.6 per cent, a rate which was acceptable.

In spite of the efforts made to mark the targets, far too many bombers were still dropping their bombs on the dummy targets prepared by the enemy. Bennett asked Harris if he might permit selected Pathfinder crews to use radio telephony to direct the bomber stream towards the correct target but this suggestion was emphatically rejected. At the beginning of September, whilst the Pathfinders were still dependent on their primitive equipment and visual methods to find targets, a mistake occurred which reinforced the criticism that if the wrong target was marked the entire main force would be misled into bombing the wrong place. On this occasion the target was Saarbrücken. The line of approach took the bomber stream along the valley over Saarlauten, and one Pathfinder aircraft dropped his markers over that town. The other markers had continued their flight to the correct target, but inevitably the main weight of bombs was directed on Saarlauten. Fortunately, it was itself a useful target with a complex distribution of industry. Harris was very understanding and made the observation that the Pathfinders had at least bombed a target, as opposed to a haphazard unloading of bombs over a wide area.

Whilst Lovell and the boffins at Defford were trying to improve the serviceability and picture quality of H_2S, Bennett was able in December, 1942, to use another new device called Oboe on Pathfinder operations. The inventors, Jones and Reeves, were under his operational control. Their equipment was mostly hand-made and was installed on the aircraft by squadron personnel. This system depended upon two stations in England which sent out radar pulses to the aircraft. One station sent a signal with dots on one side and dashes on the other to indicate whether the aircraft was maintaining the required course to bring it to the target. The other station sent warning signals to the aircraft as it approached the target and finally a long dash to indicate to the crew the moment when the target markers or bombs should be released.

The theoretical accuracy of Oboe was very high, although

*Air Vice Marshal Bennett
in 8 Group operations
room.* Bennett family

initially one of its limitations was that only two aircraft could be
directed at the same time. Its range was also limited but did cover
the whole of the Ruhr. The great value of Oboe was its accuracy
and independence of weather; targets could be sky marked when
they were totally covered by thick cloud. This was done for the first
time over Düsseldorf on 31st December, 1942, when two Mosquitoes acted as markers and eight Lancasters bombed. Although a
gale sweeping England brought down the mast of one of the Oboe
stations, the results of the bombing so impressed Harris that he
ordered a raid on Essen, one of the most important targets in
Germany. During January, 1943, a bad month for weather, when
without blind marking Bomber Command would have been totally
ineffective, up to seventy Lancasters were employed, against Essen
six times and against Duisburg twice. What was particularly
gratifying to Bennett was that although the sky marking Mosquitoes had to fly absolutely level on a straight course of fifty miles
towards the target, making them an easier prey for night fighters
and ground gunners, not one of them was lost in the course of 106
sorties up to the end of February.

Equally gratifying was the raid on Essen on 9th January, when
the city was totally covered by cloud. The Krupps works was one of
the most important enemy targets and the German authorities had
to accept that it was being attacked by a blind bombing method,
although Hitler refused to believe that such a thing was possible. In

Bennett's opinion, Oboe made possible the destruction not only of Germany's industrial capacity but also of German morale. He considered it to be the most effective single weapon in Britain's entire armoury. Equally, he deplored the fact that the names of the inventors, Jones and Reeves, were scarcely known to the British public. Neither they nor any of their team ever received any honours for their enormous contribution towards victory.

Until H_2S was ready for fitting to Pathfinder aircraft, Bennett still had to use visual methods for finding and marking aiming points when the targets were beyond the range of Oboe. The target finding tactics that he employed began with the despatch of the best crews to drop a considerable load of flares over the aiming point. These "Finders" were accompanied by "Supporters". The "Illuminators" would follow to put a stick of flares across the aiming point. Next came the "Primary Markers", the most accurate bomb aimers, who dropped Target Indicators over the stick of flares. Last came the "Backers up", adding further Target Indicators so that the main force of bombers had a mark to continue to aim at throughout the duration of the attack. Bennett had begun to experiment with different permutations of marking and illuminating in September, 1942, and the following month he had invited the Bomber Command groups to attend a meeting at Wyton to comment upon his methods. The innovations were favourably received by most main force crews, who liked to be led.

In the first months of Pathfinder operations, inaccurate wind forecasts resulted in the "Finders" arriving early or late over the aiming points. It did not matter much if they were late, as the main force bombers would also be late, but an early arrival and poor timing of the marking resulted in disappointing results in the effectiveness of the bombing. Bennett's solution was to allow an additional minute per hour to the time estimated for the run to the target to ensure that the Pathfinders arrived on time; any earliness could be lost by a timed dog-leg during the latter part of the flight. Furthermore, to impress upon crews the importance of accuracy, Bennett insisted that the time each aircraft dropped its load of markers or bombs should be logged to an accuracy of ten seconds.

By the beginning of 1943, Pathfinder Force had the crews, Oboe, H_2S, useful pyrotechnics and valuable experience. Bomber Command had become more effective and Winston Churchill had begun to regain his faith in the bomber offensive. Bennett was aware that antagonism within Bomber Command had still to be expected but he was confident of even better results in the future. Harris thought so too; Bennett was promoted to air commodore and Pathfinder Force became a separate Group. He owed this to the Commander in Chief, who "fought the bureaucrats who wanted some senior senile stooge to command it".

The Battle of Berlin   6

PATHFINDER FORCE squadrons had at first been stationed at airfields under the control of a more senior officer. Bennett had originally been allotted a staff of only four officers and a WAAF corporal. Upgraded to the status of group, however, appointments of a senior air staff officer and a senior administration officer had to be made. The first of these posts was filled by a former fellow pilot (both had served on RAF flying boats). Of this officer Bennett wrote, "He was a solid type and in spite of an air which was casual at times he was in general a very conscientious officer. He did not always agree with my ideas or policies but he served me well enough and stayed with me until the end of the war." This was Group Captain (later Air Commodore) Boyce. Finding a senior administration officer who was both willing to undertake such an un-warlike task in the middle of war and who had the qualities necessary to serve those who were fighting was more difficult. Three officers filled this post before Bennett could record that he "finished up on the best of terms with Group Captain Mc. C. White, who did a grand job and produced efficiency with the right spirit."

As group engineering officer, Bennett had the services of Sarsby, who after the war followed him into British South American Airways and then Airflight. Together they introduced a system of planned maintenance long before other groups in either Bomber or Coastal Command, so that at any one time two aircraft were withdrawn for servicing while the remaining sixteen in the squadron were available for operations. Serviceability of Pathfinder aircraft, despite a high damage rate, was kept at a very satisfactory level. Bennett and Sarsby were also able to achieve standardisation of aircraft; having begun Pathfinder operations with four different types they hoped to reduce the number to two, Lancasters and Mosquitoes.

There were two civilians at Bennett's HQ. The first of these was the group meteorology officer. Initially, confusion was caused by the variety of forecasts issued by the officers attached to the different Groups; ultimately they were required to confer over the telephone to co-ordinate their views. The other civilian represented the Operational Research section, a scientist whose job it was to investigate the results of bombing from a scientific point of view, passing the information on to the Air Ministry. Bennett made it clear to his researcher that he was there to help win the war and not simply to record its progress. He was given the job of attending to mathematical calculations, particularly in respect of Oboe, and he proved to be a valuable asset. Other researchers in Bennett's experience "did tend to have preconceived views and then set out to prove those ideas regardless of whether they were right or wrong. There is no doubt that when a scientist is determined to prove something it is extremely difficult to stop him."

The recognition of the valuable work that Pathfinder Force had done made Bennett much more optimistic about the future effectiveness of Bomber Command. All too soon, however, he was dismayed by the diversion of the Command's efforts from striking at the heart of Germany to other targets which in his view were a waste not only of effort but of crews and aircraft. There had been a vast expenditure of bombs directed at the *Scharnhorst* and *Gneisenau* at Brest before these two vessels had escaped unscathed through the Channel.

Bennett himself had been lucky not to lose his life in attempts to destroy the *Tirpitz* in Trondheim. Concern about losses of merchant shipping had resulted in Bomber Command being ordered to attack the submarine pens in St Nazaire and Lorient. These pens were protected by solid concrete five metres thick and no bombs were capable of penetrating them. This was explained to

The German warship Tirpitz *in a fjord near Trondheim, Norway, 1942.* RAF Museum

the Admiralty, who still insisted upon the attacks. The submarine crews were not accommodated in either St Nazaire or Lorient but at a safe distance away from them. During the first few months of 1943 an enormous weight of bombs was dropped on these two ports and Bennett was scathing in his condemnation. "Totally ineffective from the point of view of the submarine campaign, it did a great deal to harm our political position with the French people. It was total and wanton destructiveness of the cities of our ally and did no good whatever." From the point of view of the enemy these attacks provided welcome relief to the people of Germany.

Bennett considered that the bombing of a German target on one single occasion was the equivalent of going through the Battle of Jutland or any other great naval battle. In one tour of duty a main force bomber crew experienced thirty such battles, and in either of the other two services one bomber raid would be considered as the experience of a lifetime. Nor was danger to be expected only from the enemy. Bennett contended, "The battle commenced almost as soon as one had taken off. First of all there was the danger of being mis-identified by some friendly fighter, particularly those manned by our gallant allies, who were so trigger happy that it was unbelievable. Then as we were climbing over our own coast it was almost certain that some odd trawlers or naval units would immediately open up and blaze away at us as we went past. The fact that we might be going west to east just after sunset, quite clearly indicating that we were friendly, plus all the elaborate warning organisations for notifying naval units of our activities, apparently made no difference. They fired away and quite frequently hit us." The homeward journey from a raid not only brought continued attention to the bomber crews from night fighters and anti-aircraft fire but "the chances of a reception from the friendly ships in the Channel was always with one."

By April, 1943, when Bomber Command was once again concentrating its main efforts against the industrial areas of German cities, Hitler had reacted to the increased threat from accurate bombing. Priority in aircraft construction was being switched from bombers to fighters: the German night fighter force which before the emergence of the Pathfinders had consisted of a few hundred aircraft had increased to 1,500 and that number was rising. They were backed by a more elaborate system of radar together with a greater number of guns. Yet by constantly changing his tactics Bennett was able to keep the losses of Pathfinder aircraft relatively low.

He had been more than satisfied with the performance of the Mosquitoes and procured others. On Oboe operations, two Mosquito squadrons were employed in sufficient strength to do all the marking required by Bomber Command. A third Mosquito squadron was used to go in with the early markers and also to carry out diversionary attacks in order to attract night fighters away from the main force. The fighters might be lured sixty or seventy miles from the principal target before their ground controllers became aware that they had been deceived. Bennett also devised a tactic of nuisance raids with targets of his own choice to confuse the enemy, and although Harris only became aware of this some time after their initiation he thoroughly approved. Losses of Mosquitoes were so small that Bennett successfully applied for more; thanks to their simple wood construction they could be produced at a high rate. Eventually Pathfinder Force had nine Mosquito squadrons, and Bennett ran his own crew conversion unit and a maintenance unit.

The losses of heavy aircraft were greater, bringing the group's overall losses to average out at between $3\frac{1}{2}$ and 5 per cent each month. Unlike Harris, who seldom visited the airfields where the bomber squadrons were stationed, Bennett always had a telephone briefing conference with his squadron commanders before they in turn briefed their squadrons. Each night he visited one or more of the airfields to be present at the de-briefing of crews on their return from operations.

Squadron Leader Ivor Broom, commanding a flight of 128 Squadron, was detailed to lead a formation of a number of Mosquito squadrons on a daylight formation bombing attack from 26,000 feet against Duisburg. After studying his orders he decided that the speeds stipulated were too slow for satisfactory formation flying. Accordingly he gave his navigator a higher speed to use for flight planning but so arranged the flight plan that he would arrive at each squadron rendezvous point at the correct time and would drop his bombs on time. The raid was successful but on entering the de-briefing room at Wyton he was astonished to be berated by a very angry group commander. "Why did you not fly at the speeds I laid down?" Bennett demanded and, before Broom could offer an explanation, "I was following you in my Beaufighter and I couldn't keep up with you!"

Inevitably there were some among those who failed to return whom Bennett regarded as good friends, and it came as a personal blow when one of these was a Pathfinder who had served most of his operational tour. Bennett later confessed, "This naturally had its effects on one's nerves and spirits and occasionally driving home from interrogation in the early hours of the morning it was hard to avoid breaking down and shedding a few tears, which was probably a good safety valve in any case. To have this constant strain over such a long period, night after night and month after month, had its wearing effect however tough one tried to make oneself superficially."

Some officers close to Bennett thought him a reserved man who adopted a brusque manner to mask his personal feelings. He felt obliged to make an example of those who failed to meet his standards. A crew were ordered to be off their station and out of 8 Group by 10.00 am when they admitted to dropping their markers downwind instead of upwind. After a raid on Montdidier which was scheduled to last three minutes Bennett had four crews on the carpet, three for being three minutes late, a fourth for being eleven minutes late. A raid on Pilsen in May, 1943, was a failure, most of the bombs having been dropped on a neighbouring town. The following day Bennett summoned many of his crews to Wyton, having personally scrutinised each navigator's log to discover where mistakes had been made.

Yet Bennett identified himself with the Pathfinders and any reflection on their reputation he took as a personal insult. He would defend any one of them against the most powerful accuser outside 8 Group. Some group commanders ordered former members of Pathfinder Force to remove their eagle badge and had to be reminded that the King had approved it. Bennett's crews held him in enormous respect for his professional competence and he had their complete confidence however intolerant and hard to please they found him. His great responsibilities allowed him neither the time nor the inclination to make himself a popular figure.

Perhaps it was more surprising that the man whose keen analytical brain could speedily master the most complicated invention devised by scientists also readily accepted the existence of supernatural forces. In Canada when a Hudson had been reported missing en route to Gander, Bennett recalled a number of occasions from his past experience in aviation when in such circumstances telepathic messages had been passed to a wife or close relative by a survivor. He had unhesitatingly telephoned to the pilot's wife and asked her whether she believed him to be alive. Her conviction that this was so had spurred his endeavours to effect a rescue. When his current group navigation officer had failed to return from a raid it came as a shock to Bennett when this officer appeared to be present in his office. In fact, he was confronted by the man's twin brother, who had been serving with Coastal Command in Iceland when he had received a telepathic message. His CO had accepted his request for leave and facilitated his return to England to comfort his parents. Having assured them that their son was alive and uninjured, he had reported to Pathfinder HQ to pass on the good news. Bennett observed that "this was truly a wonderful example of the powers of telepathy at a time of great human stress."

During the early summer of 1943, Pathfinders used Oboe on

Ruhr targets and H_2S to mark Berlin, Hamburg and other German cities. The success of the raids was recognised by the Russians, who were helped to save Stalingrad from capture through the inability of the Germans to supply their forces with enough heavy equipment. After the war, Hitler's industry minister Albert Speer blamed Germany's failure to supply sufficient anti-tank guns to the eastern front on the need to deploy 20,000 anti-aircraft guns against Allied bombers. For his contribution, Bennett was awarded the Order of Alexander Nevsky. At the end of July, the Pathfinders marked Hamburg using H_2S and were followed by almost 800 heavy aircraft, whose bombs struck their targets with devastating effect. The following night Essen was the target but Bennett sent a few Mosquitoes to Hamburg to "keep their nerves on edge." Twenty-four hours later the city was again the principal target, followed next day by more Mosquito attacks. A day later the job was finished, with 75 per cent of Hamburg destroyed. Bennett tried to persuade Harris to use his influence with the government to take "appropriate political action" to encourage peace feelers from Germany. "It was an opportunity", he wrote, "which we missed."

It was at this time that a counter-measure code-named "Window" was used against German radar stations. This was the ejection from aircraft of strips of aluminium foil cut to correspond to the wavelength of the German radar. They filled the radar screens with responses, making it impossible to differentiate between the aircraft and "Window". This idea bought a little peace for markers' crews trying to make an accurate run to the aiming point. Pathfinders also used it to good effect when they tried to give the impression of a large bomber force en route to a target other than the true one. Bennett sometimes wondered to what extent it was appreciated that unarmed Mosquito crews were deliberately enticing fighters on themselves to protect the main force.

Pathfinder Force continued to grow as squadrons were detached from other groups in the Command. Bennett faced an awkward problem when he was asked to incorporate an entire Australian squadron. He refused point blank, to the surprise of the Australians. He had insisted from the outset that each crew would have to meet his standards and he was able to maintain that principle to the end.

The value of the Force to both Bomber Command and the total war effort was reflected in the appearance at Bennett's HQ of distinguished visitors. Among these Mrs Ogden Reid of *The New York Herald Tribune* was taken by Bennett to the end of the runway to watch a squadron of Mosquitoes take off in quick succession for a raid on Berlin. Bad weather had caused the cancellation of all heavy bomber operations, and looking at the small twin engined machines manned by a crew of two Mrs Reid enquired how heavy a bomb load they could carry. Being informed that each aircraft carried a 4,000 lb blockbuster she asked how that compared with the B-17 Flying Fortress then being flown by American bomber crews on daylight operations. When it was explained that the B-17 with its large crew of air gunners carried a lighter bomb load Mrs Reid was taken aback and expressed to Bennett the hope that the American public would remain in ignorance of the fact.

As a group commander, Bennett inevitably incurred many administrative duties that he found irksome, but at least he could deal with some of these in a manner that differed markedly from that of other senior officers with much longer RAF service who had been brought up in a different mould. When interviewing men recommended for a commission he adopted the principle that the first essential of a good officer was efficiency and therefore a thorough knowledge of his own job. His questions ranged over the candidate's qualities from that aspect and he did not concern himself with social background and the type of school the man had once attended.

Bennett grew increasingly impatient with the RAF Police who harrassed and victimised his air crew members over minor infractions of service rules. He had to remind the provost marshal that it was no part of his duty to make life more irksome for those who were doing the actual fighting. On one of his unannounced visits to a station commander he arrived as an airman was already in front of his CO on a charge of walking across the grass to a hangar, contrary to Station Standing Orders. Bennett interrupted to enquire whether this was the most direct route and on being informed that it was, he "let it be known emphatically that if anybody . . . walked any other way than by the straightest possible line between the places in which he had to work he would be on a charge of sabotaging the war effort".

This conflict with the Establishment mentality also erupted at his own HQ station—Wyton. Bennett wanted the massive brick structure of a rifle range demolished because an aircraft which swung off the runway after landing due to damage or a wounded pilot could collide with the structure and endanger life. His request was refused by the Works and Building Department, then by Bomber Command's administrative section and finally by the Air Ministry. Thoroughly disgusted, Bennett ordered the demolition on his own authority and had the site levelled and rolled. Subsequently he saw disabled aircraft on two occasions pass over the exact spot where the range had been. "In both cases it would have meant the loss of all on board, one a Lancaster and one a Mosquito."

As the Commander in Chief, Bomber Command, had

anticipated, the creation of Pathfinder Force whose succsss had elevated it to the status of a Group caused jealousy at more than one level. Bennett took the view that having been given the job of marking the target it followed that he should have the responsibility for choosing the route to reach it. He did not want the bombers of other groups to be equipped with H_2S because he anticipated that their crews would disregard the markers and attempt to identify targets on their own. Being the only group commander with experience of current bomber operations he became impatient if his recommendations were disputed when they all met to discuss tactics before a raid. He referred to those group commanders who opposed his views as "the unruly barons of Bomber Command."

Bennett got on well with Air Vice Marshal Carr commanding 4 Group but his relations with some of the others were strained. Air Vice Marshal Coryton had been "openly antagonistic" to the Pathfinder concept, although Bennett regarded him as an excellent group commander. Coryton was relieved of his command of 5 Group when he declined an order from Harris to send a mere twelve Lancasters to bomb Berlin. He had protested that he could not justifiably expose so small a force to the concentrated attention of the defences. Air Vice Marshal Cochrane accepted this order and promptly replaced Coryton at 5 Group. In a professional sense Cochrane became the bête noir of Bennett. The former had known the Commander in Chief for a much longer period, having been a flight commander in 1922 when both officers had flown Victoria troop transports. Harris regarded Cochrane "as a genius . . . a really outstanding commander". Bennett held a contrary opinion. He attributed to Cochrane the single pilot policy which had been adopted when the latter had been Director of Training Flying; but what was particularly galling was that Harris permitted Cochrane to pursue an independent role in marking targets assigned to 5 Group. Bennett acknowledged the ardour and zeal of Cochrane and conceded that he had a magnificent brain but "had he had the experience behind it the results would have been wholly exceptional . . . if Ralph Cochrane had been given the opportunity to operate as a captain of a heavy bomber for fifteen or twenty raids he would have been a wonderful group commander."

The Honourable Sir Ralph Cochrane was a cousin of the 13th Earl of Dundonald and a descendant of Admiral Lord Cochrane, one of Lord Nelson's commanders, whose tomb is in Westminister Abbey. Joining the Royal Navy in 1907, he had served as a midshipman at the outbreak of the First World War before transferring in 1915 to the airship branch of the Royal Naval Air Service. In 1920, by which time he was a Flight Lieutenant in the Royal Air Force, he took the advice of Sir Hugh Trenchard and

gave up airships for aeroplanes. He joined the squadron commanded by Harris in Iraq, which was engaged in the new policy of keeping rebellious tribesmen under control by threat of air strike against their villages. At a time when the British Government was committed to a policy of disarmament it was not an easy task for an ambitious officer to distinguish himself but Cochrane did so. Arriving in New Zealand as a mere wing commander in 1936 to advise the Labour Government how to form an air force on a budget of five million pounds, Cochrane was invited to remain and became the first Chief of Air Staff of the RNZAF. He stayed until

1939, when he was appointed ADC to King George VI. This was a very different background from that of the young man from Australia who had left the RAF in 1935 with the rank of flying officer and rejoined only in 1941. Many years younger than other senior officers holding the same rank, Bennett was very easily exasperated by their style of leadership.

Since 1939, secret work being undertaken by the Germans at Peenemünde on the Baltic coast had been under investigation by British intelligence. In June, 1943, Dr R. V. Jones, the distinguished physicist at the head of the scientific intelligence unit in the Air Ministry, convinced Lord Cherwell that the aerial photographs taken showing several apparent rockets were not a deliberate hoax. Soon afterwards the War Cabinet were warned that work on the V2 rocket with a range of between 100 and 200 miles was in progress there. Bennett learnt from Lord Cherwell that the Government was sufficiently worried about this and other secret weapons to make Peenemünde a priority target. Harris arranged a full scale Bomber Command attack by 600 heavy aircraft with precision marking assigned to Cochrane's 5 Group. He did insist, however, that Bennett should choose a master bomber to assist in directing the attack. The nature and position of the particular buildings to be destroyed meant that the raid would have to be carried out on a bright moonlight night with good visibility.

The task of the master bomber was to stay over the target during the whole attack and using radio telephony warn crews to ignore misplaced flares or decoy fires lit by the Germans. He would assess the accuracy of the bombing and broadcast in a calm and reassuring voice advice to the bomber crews approaching the target area. Bennett's request to use radio telephony at the inception of Pathfinder Force had met with a refusal by Harris, who subsequently changed his mind when the same suggestion came from Cochrane. The latter had then authorised Guy Gibson to pioneer the master bomber technique when 617 Squadron was formed to attack the Möhne and Eder dams. The Peenemünde raid was a great success, severely damaging the rocket factories and killing a number of scientists. Good use was made of "Window" and tactical routeing. The German controllers were kept guessing the intended target, expecting an attack first on Kiel, then Berlin, Rostock, Swinemünde and Stettin. The raid delayed the V2 offensive by at least three months, preventing the use of the new weapons against the invasion beaches.

During the summer of 1943, Bennett wrote to Harris complaining that the standard of crews being posted to 8 Group was falling. This followed reports that markers had been badly placed during raids on Hanover. The other Groups, reluctant to

PEENEMUNDE. 26.7.43 N/890. 1154 to 1159 inclusive. Height - 28 to 29,500'.
Pilot - S/Ldr. G.E.Hughes, DFC₂. Observer - F/O Chubb, DFM. F.L. 36".
Radio and Aircraft Factory: Before attack.

Above: *German secret weapons factory photographed before an RAF attack, July, 1943.* RAF Museum

Left: *Peenemunde after the RAF bombing.* RAF Museum

81

lose their most experienced crews, were refusing applications from these but transferring men who had not volunteered for the Pathfinder Force and others who had made a nuisance of themselves. One third of the crews were arriving as complete freshmen and the average Pathfinder captain had completed only twenty sorties. There was not enough time to train the new crews, especially as they were required to convert to a different type of aircraft and to familiarise themselves with H_2S. Bennett also pointed out that H_2S sets needed to be improved both in serviceability and in picture quality. In vast built-up areas the picture was not clear enough to distinguish lakes, rivers and open spaces so that the targets could be identified. He knew that Harris was on the point of ordering a prolonged series of air raids on Berlin and most of these would be made when the city was totally covered in cloud.

The poor serviceability of the H_2S sets was also causing considerable concern to Bernard Lovell. Consequently he gained the enthusiastic support of Bennett for a clandestine plan to equip six of the Pathfinder Force Lancasters with an improved set and to by-pass the official channels in order to avoid long delays. In his diary Lovell wrote, "Arrangements were made to fix the opposition and the plan was not announced until it was already started." The Lancaster had never been designed to take H_2S but "after a disappointing beginning six were equipped with the improved set and when Harris finally authorised the work to begin it was already nearing completion."

The Battle of Berlin, which opened on 18th November, 1943, was intended to be the climax of the bomber offensive. Harris had told Churchill that with the co-operation of the United States Air Force it would cost up to 500 Allied aircraft but would cost Germany the war. The directive to begin the continuous bombing of Berlin came from the Prime Minister, whose public pronouncements to this effect eliminated any element of surprise and made the task of Bomber Command more difficult. Both before and after the formation of Pathfinder Force, Berlin had been attacked by a modest number of bombers on various occasions. The great distance of Berlin from English bomber stations required the aircraft to cross a large area of enemy territory defended by searchlights, guns and fighters. This was to be an operation conducted throughout the winter when the weather was bad.

"This battle", Bennett wrote, "was indeed the bitterest part of the war for me, for not only was it gravely important that we should succeed and thereby confirm the effects of Hamburg but also it was bitter because of the great losses which we suffered. So far as the Pathfinder Force was concerned these losses were particularly serious because they included a large proportion of very experienced and good Pathfinder crews. I lost a number of squadron commanders and senior flight commanders and at one stage I thought that the backbone of the Pathfinder Force was broken."

Flying for many hours in sub-zero temperatures, many airmen suffered frostbite; when the aircraft entered cloud, the guns and gun turrets froze. The maximum weight of the Lancaster bomber had been deliberately increased by 3,000 lb in order to accommodate a heavier bomb load and the effect was to degrade its performance, making searchlight avoidance or evasive action in the face of fighter attack more difficult. Many crews were observed to be dropping their heaviest bomb, the "cookie" into the North Sea en route to the target in order to give themselves a reserve of speed and the ability to gain height. There was no doubt in the minds of those who observed this because the "cookie" could not be dropped "safe"—it always exploded. Then, having lost confidence in their

Avro Lancaster.
Imperial War Museum

83

aircraft, many pilots—including those who had jettisoned part of their bomb load—released the remainder short of the target and flew home. Among these "fringe merchants" were crews who had only to survive a few more raids to complete their operational tour. When Bennett was informed that bombs were being wasted in this way he flew out himself to verify the facts. Harris, however, would not listen to his complaints that the Lancaster was being overloaded at the expense of performance and did not believe that bomber crews would act in the manner described to him.

On the night of 1st January, 1944, more than 13 per cent of Pathfinder aircraft failed to return, but with bitter losses in tough conditions they slogged on, unable to get photographic evidence of the results at the time because all the raids were carried out when Berlin was obscured by cloud. When it was possible for reconnaissance aircraft to bring back photographs, the Air Ministry was reported to be disappointed with the results of the bombing, as was Harris. "What he did not seem to realise," wrote Bennett, "was that what I had been saying throughout the whole series of attacks was perfectly true, however unpalatable it might be." Taught that height was essential to their own safety the pilots had tried to obtain it at all costs, and the rate of climb of a normally loaded Lancaster was already too slow to give much confidence to the crews. "The captains concerned felt justified in acting in this way as they were quite unable to climb and were apprehensive of icing in the clouds ahead. In their view it was a question of necessity . . . the net result was that of the bombs which left England a very large proportion did not reach Berlin."

Some of the boffins joined the argument and criticised both Harris and the Pathfinders for not using the H_2S to the best advantage when blind bombing was being undertaken. Harris was outraged at being criticised by those by who did not know all the facts. Inaccurate forecasting of upper winds had sometimes resulted in the main force failing to arrive within the limited time necessary after the release of markers. Harris called the boffins "a bunch of pimply prima donnas struggling to get into the limelight". He told the Air Ministry to order them to "mind their own bloody business."

During the winter bombing compaign against Berlin, Pathfinder Force not only participated in the sixteen major raids but on sixteen further nights Mosquitoes were sent in to maintain the attack. Despite the defences, the weather and the failure to drop many bombs on the intended targets, about 5,500 acres of Berlin were devastated. But whereas Harris had predicted the loss of up to 500 bombers the true figure turned out to be 1,047, with a further 1,682 returning damaged, of which 100 were destroyed on landing.

All-Weather Operations   7

DURING THE WINTER campaign against Berlin, Bennett received a visit from the Minister of Petroleum Warfare, Geoffrey Lloyd, and two advisers, bringing with them a letter from the Prime Minister to explain their presence. Briefly, the letter said that the scientists had devised a method to disperse fog from the runway area in order to allow aircraft to land. Lloyd said that the Commander in Chief, Bomber Command, was enthusiastic about the idea but as it had no special significance to the role of the Pathfinders had sent the team to the main force groups first. The reception to their invention had filled the scientists with dismay and disappointment.

"I was simply staggered at the idea of the possibilities of such a device," Bennett recalled, "and I said so in no uncertain terms." He invited his visitors to dinner and over the meal he listened to their proposals and to the requirements that they laid down for the airfield on which their experiment should be attempted. All the other groups had found excuses to account for their inability to offer any co-operation, but Bennett wasted no time in nominating Graveley as a suitable aerodrome and when he was asked to suggest a convenient time for an inspection he said, "Immediately." He was also most impressed by the way the scientists set about the installation of their equipment, laying burners along 1,000 yards of the approach area to the runway and also along the first 1,000 yards of the runway itself. The principle upon which the system worked was that the intense heat from clear burner flames cut a chasm through the fog which could be seen from above. The aircraft could descend towards the chasm and land on the runway.

Bennett needed to satisfy himself that it would be practical to land down the centre line of such an inferno. He took a Lancaster from Oakington over to Graveley at night to observe whether the intense heat and the glare from the flames would allow him to go through with the experiments, but despite this glare and some turbulence he maintained, "it was nothing to worry about . . . I did the first landing with 'Fido' burning." Bennett strongly recommended the adoption of the system and had it installed at another Pathfinder airfield—Downham Market. He wrote, "I made it a rule that whenever I wished to fly I did so regardless of the weather on the basis that 'Fido' was always there to save my miserable neck

should the need arise." One night Bennett was flying himself back to Graveley in a Beaufighter when most of England was becoming shrouded in fog. Fido was in use but there was a wind blowing across the runway, which had the effect of cutting a chasm in the fog that was not vertical but at an angle of fifty degrees. Bennett found that it was possible to make a slanting approach on to the runway before landing normally. Towards the end of the burners the aircraft was enveloped in fog and he asked the flying control officer to send out a vehicle to guide him along the taxiway. Confusion arose because the roar of the burners had drowned the sound of the Beaufighter's throttled engines and the controller at the end of the runway had not been able to see the aircraft approaching and was unaware that it was already safely on the ground.

Thereafter Bennett operated the Mosquito squadrons even when fog was forecast, restricting the number to allow his Fido-equipped airfields to cope with arrivals. In the event they attracted aircraft from other units like bees to a honey pot. The Prime Minister was delighted with the initiative shown by Bennett and the success of the experiment. Fido provided some unexpected benefits; on one occasion the pilot of a German Junkers 88 landed at Woodbridge aerodrome under the impression that he had found an airfield free from fog in Holland. His night fighter was fitted with new radar equipment for tracking British bombers. On another occasion, fog over a wide area was forecast for the period when the bombers were expected back from that night's operations. At Graveley, however, the Standard Beam approach was unserviceable, the fault being diagnosed by a corporal as a defective modulator unit. When Bennett became aware of this he telephoned to the station commander from Group Headquarters and urged him to do whatever was necessary to have the SBA serviceable in time for the bombers to guide themselves along the beam to Graveley and thereby to land with the help of Fido. The nearest spare modulator unit was held in store 150 miles away but the station commander and the station signals officer set off together in an Anson to bring back the necessary part, anxiously hoping that the diagnosis of the corporal was correct. At four o'clock in the morning Bennett appeared at Graveley whilst the spare part was being installed, and to the relief of all, the familiar dots and dashes could be heard once more.

As the Battle of Berlin was coming to a close Harris telephoned to Bennett to ask for his opinion on a new way of marking targets in the city. It emanated from Cochrane, who had clearly persuaded the Commander in Chief that marking could be done by Mosquitoes flown at fifty feet above the roof tops to find and mark the aiming points. Bennett objected on several counts. First, with the prevailing winter weather Target Indicators would not be seen through the clouds by the bomber crews. Secondly, as a former fighter pilot of 29 squadron at North Weald and from his considerable experience on subsequent occasions, he was quite convinced that it was impossible to map-read over a densely built-up area at low level. With a field of view limited to a few hundred yards in an aircraft travelling at 200 knots, identification would have to be made within a second or two. The method would be excellent for many targets but not within Berlin; the Mosquitoes would be annihilated.

Harris was considerably put out by this flat condemnation of Cochrane's plan, which had gained his own approval. Thirty minutes after the conclusion of this telephone conversation Bennett received a message to report in person to the Commander in Chief at Bomber Command HQ in High Wycombe. He flew as far as Halton in an old Hurricane, one of the aircraft which he used as a hack, and was then driven to HQ "to be received with a frigid and formal notification" that he was immediately to send 83 and 97 Squadrons together with one Mosquito squadron to 5 Group, which would in future adopt the low level marking method and would mark a large number of their own targets themselves.

"This was in itself a tremendous slap in the face to a Force which had turned Bert Harris' Bomber Command from a wasteful and ineffective force into a mighty and successful one", Bennett complained. He feared that the rest of Bomber Command would interpret the detachment of the three squadrons as an indication of a loss of confidence by the Commander in Chief in the performance of Pathfinder Force. To rub salt in the wound Bennett was ordered to give initial training to crews before they were assigned to the control of Cochrane. Throughly incensed, he rang Saundby, Senior Air Staff Officer at Bomber Command, to complain at such treatment, but "he simply shrugged his shoulders and said that he and Cochrane had once been flight commanders together under Bert Harris in the Middle East and that the same situation had prevailed. Cochrane could do anything and the Commander in Chief would always support him. Any attempts to convince the Commander in Chief that Cochrane could ever be wrong were doomed to failure." Saundby's conviction that it would be hopeless to pursue the matter further provoked Bennett into enquiring where he would get any more Mosquitoes when those employed on Cochrane's schemes were all shot down.

When 97 Squadron arrived at their new station under Cochrane's control they were treated to a terse lecture from the station commander to the effect that they could forget about their former methods and would have to adopt those devised by 5 Group. "We are fighting the Germans, Sir", a voice called out, "not 5 Group." The intense loyalty which the Pathfinder squadrons thus removed from his control still retained towards their former group was a source of some comfort to Bennett. His problems were however increased because the Pathfinders still had as much marking to do as in the past, with fewer crews and aircraft—a quarter of his Lancasters had been transferred. Furthermore, to reduce the losses of aircraft Harris varied his tactics: the bomber force might be divided to attack two different targets, or a particular target might be attacked in two phases. From a defensive point of view this made sound sense but it meant that the Pathfinder Force was sorely pressed to find enough aircraft to mark the targets and perform their other duties. Sometimes the Commander in Chief specified four targets in the course of one night; when these were out of Oboe range the Mosquitoes could not be used for marking and the job fell to the depleted number of Lancasters.

The decison of Harris to encourage Cochrane in the development of pathfinding and bombing techniques independently was not due to dissatisfaction with the results achieved by Bennett. The Commander in Chief had never wanted to have this function performed by a corps d'élite and had always hoped to see new methods tried out by other groups. The Air Ministry had forced his hand in the matter and in face of Bennett's flat rejection of Cochrane's suggestion of precision attacks Harris was determined to allow the experiment to go ahead. The various techniques developed during 1944 by 5 Group owed much to Group Captain Leonard Cheshire, whose exploits earned him the VC, DSO and DFC. Cheshire had after his third tour of operations applied to join Pathfinder Force, but when Bennett told him that he would be accepted if he could prove his flying to be of the required standard, Cheshire felt rebuffed and recalled later, "I told him that if that was the case I would see if I could find somewhere else to go." The precision attacks carried out by 5 Group were always at the mercy of the weather and their main successes were when the target was clear. Probably what had made Harris adopt the new initiative was the success of Cheshire in marking an aircraft factory at Toulouse which his own Lancaster squadron then bombed with unprecedented accuracy from their normal height.

Wing Commander Cheshire, master bomber of 5 Group, Bomber Command.
RAF Museum

Low level precision marking was never tried on Berlin. "Fortunately for Cochrane", wrote Bennett, "that battle had come to an end before he was in a position to try his methods on it." During the remainder of 1944, 5 Group sometimes participated with the rest of Bomber Command's main force but also attacked a large number of targets on their own. Resentful of the loss of three squadrons to Cochrane's group, Bennett carefully analysed the results of this rival's activities. Many of the targets were small and undefended, while "very mediocre results" were obtained from attacks on Munich, Brunswick and Wilhelmshaven. On their first big raid on Munich, 5 Group's master bomber with three other Mosquito pilots to back him up "tried gallantly for nearly twenty minutes to get his markers on the correct aiming point", failing to do so for the reasons predicted by Bennett. It was left to a Pathfinder Force master bomber to take over and mark the aiming point by the former method in visual conditions. "From then on the raid was controlled by our master bomber with fairly good success", despite losses of bombers to the German fighters while they circled the target waiting for markers to be placed.

On 13th March, 1944, Bomber Command ordered a raid to be directed against Nuremberg, and of 795 aircraft which took part in the attack 94 failed to return. "This loss", Bennett wrote, "was considered by many at the time to be a catastrophic accident which just happened to occur . . . I believe it would be best from an historical point of view and as a lesson for the future to realise that it was caused and not simply accidental."

Saundby, deputy to the Commander in Chief, was surprised and uneasy when he observed the route chosen by Harris and his advisers, because it employed a long straight track with only one turning point to the north-east of Frankfurt before the final course towards the target. Almost as direct was the return journey. When he passed details of these routes over the telephone to Bennett the latter openly criticised them and together with his staff at 8 Group prepared an alternative plan. This was based upon their knowledge of ground defences, the German night fighter defences and a weather report just brought back by one of the group's own Mosquitoes. The Germans had found ways of isolating the effects of "Window" and it remained necessary to choose a route which would leave some doubt in enemy minds what the target might be. It had become increasingly common, since Harris had encouraged Cochrane to pursue an independent line in tactics, for the group commanders to question and to object to the routing planned by Pathfinder Head Quarters and this was to happen again. Cochrane wanted to try a novel tactic, that of sending almost every bomber on the direct track to Nuremberg. By adopting the shortest route out and home, less fuel would be needed and therefore a greater bomb load could be carried. The only diversion would be sorties by Mosquitoes against night fighter airfields and targets in the Ruhr, while fifty Halifaxes would also be used to lay mines near Heligoland. The direct route was supported by the majority of the group commanders, only Air Vice Marshal Carr preferring Bennett's plan. The Commander in Chief took the decision to adopt Cochrane's route and Saundby rang Bennett again to inform him that Harris had chosen to give the main force group commanders a chance to see whether their theories were correct. The direct route must stand.

When the squadron commanders and officers commanding stations were told the details of the routing, Bennett received a number of telephone calls expressing strong objections. Wing Commander Daniels DSO, DFC, the young officer commanding 35 Squadron, complained about the route and the absence of spoof targets. He expressed the opinion that the bombers "might suffer the greatest chop rate ever". In the event a long straight run was made towards Nuremberg without any tactical trickery. Not only did the Germans guess the target correctly but the thick cloud which had been forecast disappeared and in perfect visibility, with every bomber displaying a long white condensation trail, enemy fighters were presented with easy targets.

In the words of Bennett, "I opposed the long straight route because clearly the conditions were far too dangerous for such a course, particularly when we had been warned that there was a strong chance of there being bright moonlight. Nuremberg turned out to be a very expensive raid. I believe it would still have involved high losses even with our proposed route but certainly they would not have been as high as those which were incurred. The wind that night lost us many aircraft by blowing them over heavily defended flak belts, where they became targets for concentrated and accurate box-barrages. The good navigators discovered the true wind speed and corrected their courses. The bad navigators did not and the result was that the main force, instead of being a compact and narrow stream, was spread out to a width of about fifty miles, making interception of them by fighters easier. The dog-legs and the dummies we had proposed would have added about two per cent to the flying distance and the time in the air. That is not much, just a few minutes, and I believe this would have fooled most if not all of the German night fighter force."

Referring to the tactics employed by the Pathfinders to confuse the enemy and weaken his defensive measures, Bennett admitted that they had met with varying success but never completely failed. "I would claim that these tactics were one of the greatest contributions the Pathfinder Force made in the bomber offensive. The bright night of the Nuremberg operation made spoof targets and complex routing even more essential."

Explaining the role of the master bomber on this occasion, Daniels said, "We would arrive five minutes before anybody else. It was extremely unpleasant. Sometimes the Germans would all stay quiet hoping that you were just a stray aircraft and thinking that if they didn't open up you would pass on . But later, when they knew our technique, they would concentrate on trying to shoot down the first aircraft that moved—as they did over Nuremberg. With Bennett, of course, you weren't allowed just to carry flares. You had to have bombs, whatever else you were carrying."

Bennett flew to two Pathfinder stations as the bomber crews were returning to assess the results. At the first he reproved a squadron commander who said, "Sir, this has been the worst chop night we have ever had." At Graveley Daniels exploded, "Bloody hell: why did we have to go that way?" He reported more attacks than he had ever experienced before—never had he seen so many bombers shot down in one night. In fact it was estimated that fifty bombers never even reached Nuremberg. Of those that returned to base, twelve crashed on landing and fifty nine were badly damaged, while 545 airmen were killed. When the official history of the air offensive was written, one of the few things with which Bennett agreed was the finding that the operational planning of the raid was "uncharacteristically bad and unimaginative".

Cochrane maintained that no other route was possible with a stream of bombers spread over a fifty mile width, as alterations of course would have had to be very large. Bennett was seething. "Why the main force group commanders should be so critical and intolerant of the methods which had saved so many lives I could never quite make out, beyond the fact that it seemed merely human weakness that they should revolt against the loss of their power to a youngster in another group . . . one must remember that practically no senior officers in the RAF had any appreciable first hand operational experience in the current war and they were therefore at a grave disadvantage in any tactical planning."

The blame for this state of affairs Bennett attributed to the Prime Minister, the Cabinet and the Air Council, whose policy it was to prohibit operational flying by senior officers over enemy territory. Years later, he recalled, "It cost us thousands of lives and many failures and was in my view the most deplorable of all the mistakes which we made during the war." During that spring of 1944, the Germans were striving to pick off the leading Pathfinder aircraft and by preventing them from marking, to reduce the weight and accuracy of the bombing.

To counter the severe losses among Pathfinder crews Bennett devised a scheme whereby his Lancaster squadrons would take off after the main force and by climbing at an indicated airspeed of 155 knots instead of the usual 130 knots would overtake the main force en route and only appear in front during the last stage of the journey to the target. There was considerable scepticism among the pilots whether a Lancaster loaded to its maximum weight would achieve any rate of climb at the revised speed, and on the very first occasion when the new technique was adopted one pilot abandoned his attempt and returned to his station complaining that it was impossible to climb at 155 knots. When Bennett was informed, he ordered the pilot to be at readiness to fly the same aircraft at the same weight on the following afternoon. He appeared himself at the appointed time, said, "Good afternoon, let's go", and very shortly afterwards the Lancaster was airborne. Bennett let the speed build up to 155 knots and then climbed to 18,000 feet before returning for a landing. He had no word of criticism for the pilot and there were no subsequent recriminations; he got back into his car and drove away. It was enough to prove his point by example, and the incident exemplified the reason why he was so much admired and respected by everyone serving under him in 8 Group.

At about this time Bennett had another battle, not with his fellow group commanders but with Air Marshal Slessor, Commander in Chief Coastal Command. The subject was H$_2$S, the development of which Bennett attributed to his own enthusiasm and the co-operation offered to the scientists by Pathfinder Force. The Mark III H$_2$S was a considerable improvement on earlier versions and he looked forward to its incorporation into his group's aircraft. It had been discovered that this equipment could also be used to detect German submarines and would therefore be an extremely valuable tool for Coastal Command. Bennett took the view that the most important job of defeating Germany was being done by Bomber Command and Pathfinder Force in particular; depriving him of H_2S sets just to sink a few more U-boats would be a mistake. At the Air Ministry, he and Slessor argued their case for some hours, but in the end there was a compromise and Coastal Command obtained a considerable amount of the equipment Bennett had hoped to acquire for his own group.

Cochrane's influence over Harris continued to touch a raw nerve. Bennett was summoned to the Commander in Chief's office to listen to the commander of 5 Group explaining his plan to drop some specially heavy bombs of up to 8,000 lb close to the foundation of some lock gates damming an area of water near Hanover. The proposed raid would be carried out entirely by 5 Group, the purpose of the invitation to Bennett being to solicit the assistance of Pathfinder Force in laying flares over the targets so that 5 Group's visual markers could themselves mark the aiming point and control the raid. "I need not comment", Bennett wrote, "on the remarkable nerve of the AOC of 5 Group in asking us to co-operate, in view of the way he had treated us and weakened us both in strength and in name." Inwardly seething, Bennett continued to listen while Cheshire, commanding the squadron nominated to conduct the raid, explained that they had rejected the gyrostabilised Mark XIV bombsight, which Harris had himself sponsored and which Pathfinder Force had proved to be satisfactory, in favour of the former unstabilised Mark IX. Bennett was even more astonished when Cheshire claimed that a large number of practice bombs had been dropped from 20,000 feet with a maximum error of only twenty feet in distance and three feet in line from the target. Knowing that the ballistic error alone from that height was at least thirty or forty feet, Bennett asked Harris and Saundby whether they accepted Cheshire;s results. He reported, "They both quite solemnly agreed that they accepted them . . . in short Cochrane had mesmerised them once again and it was no use my arguing."

When the argument was about targets, however, Bennett totally supported the contention of Harris that the main weight of Bomber Command's offensive should be directed against the heart of Germany. From the time of the appointment of Harris as Commander in Chief early in 1942 there were demands that Bomber Command should switch its efforts away from Germany and give more support to the Admiralty in their struggle against U-boats and other German naval units. In fact, the claimants for the selection of targets were legion and Harris fought a constant battle against crackpots suggesting what he called "panacea" policies designed to shorten the war.

At the time, many in the RAF saw the role of the Mosquitoes as no more than nuisance raiders, whereas they inflicted a considerable amount of damage on the enemy and performed numerous different duties often at the initiative of Bennett himself. A navigator on 571 Squadron recalled that, "When the Air Vice Marshal came to brief us it would be a far more thorough and interesting briefing than normal. Afterwards, such was his confidence, he would invite anyone who wished to do so to examine his file of future targets. He would lay on a selection of three for the squadron but sometimes forget to make a final decision. Once, with take-off time fast approaching and crews and ground crews tearing their hair out, the squadron commander rang for a final decision to be told to ring later as the Air Vice Marshal was having a bath."

"A typical raid", this navigator added, "was on Hamburg. Twelve Mosquitoes approached the target from the east, dropping 'Window' to simulate a large force, and arrived over the city to drop our 4,000 lb bomb exactly three minutes before 600 heavy bombers came in from the west at the same height. Then we had to gain height as fast as possible to avoid head-on collisions and trigger-happy air gunners."

On one occasion, Bennett ordered a Mosquito squadron to approach the Great Ouse at a considerable height and when within five miles to descend rapidly so as to cross the water at a height of fifty feet and at an angle of twenty degrees. The crews did not know the ultimate purpose of this training other than that it would involve dropping something in a stretch of water. Later in the day, they were briefed for a minelaying exercise in the Kiel Canal, which connects the Baltic with all the North Sea ports. It was a very busy waterway and used by U-boats. This was a target chosen by Bennett, who telephoned to Harris for his approval and obtained it without argument. That night the squadron successfully laid the mines, effectively putting the canal out of action for over two weeks. This was despite the fact that twenty-five searchlights and almost 100 guns were available to defend it. Only one Mosquito failed to return, and Bennett was disappointed that "this little episode was not even mentioned to the British public and no honours or awards were given in relation to it."

The Mosquito meteorology flight also made a great contribution to the success of the bomber offensive. Day in, day out, in broad daylight and often in clear weather the aircraft flew deep into Germany. Flying at a great height but unarmed, the pilots had to rely on the Mosquito's ability to out-turn the enemy when intercepted by fighters. When one recalls how close to cancellation the Mosquito project came, the achievements of the aircraft in its various roles provoke both astonishment and admiration. It could carry half the load of a Lancaster, its cost was one third and it carried a crew of two instead of seven. Its casualty rate was one tenth that of the Lancaster.

Invasion and Victory   8

IN APRIL, 1944, the Supreme Allied Commander, General Eisenhower, was given control of the RAF Bomber Command with the object of obtaining a major contribution to the invasion plan. Harris viewed the plans for a land assault without enthusiasm; he could recall what had happened at Gallipoli and more recently at Dieppe. He feared that the operation might fail or, almost as serious, might achieve only a small bridgehead which would result in a stalemate and extensive diversions from the main strategic assault on Germany. Harris never deviated from the view that Bomber Command could make its greatest contribution to victory by being allowed to continue the strategic air offensive against Germany. However, once the die was cast and the British Government accepted "Overlord", Harris gave the invasion plans his full co-operation. This required Bomber Command to undertake several separate tasks before and including D-Day. The first was to destroy railway communications in France to prevent the Germans reinforcing the invasion beaches, the second was to destroy coastal radar stations to prevent the enemy observing the approach of the invasion vessels and aircraft. Finally, on D-Day itself there was to be a massive assault on German gun emplacements in the invasion areas of the French coast.

There were about 1,000 heavy aircraft engaged in the battle against German targets when, as Bennett put it, "we were diverted to other things." The first diversion requiring the participation of Pathfinder Force was the bombing of the "V"-bomb sites in the Pas-de-Calais area and some others near Cherbourg. These were permanent sites which had been constructed for the launching of 6,000 buzz-bombs a day, mainly aimed at London but also at southern targets such as Portsmouth and Southampton. Altogether sixty-four permanent sites had been identified in open country despite attempts to camouflage them.

Oboe stations had to be sited to make it possible for marker Pathfinders to be directed to the exact aiming points. Targets were attacked in daylight, and Bennett adopted a marking system of coloured smoke from candles, which were easier to see in daylight when smoke and dust from the explosion of bombs were present. Fairly small numbers of bombers were sent to each target and master bombers were used to help the main force to find the correct aiming point. So effective were the raids that Hitler had to postpone the launch date; when buzz-bombs did first appear in the

English skies they did so in far fewer numbers than had been intended. The Germans were obliged to improvise temporary sites and had frequently to move their position. This meant that supplies of V-bombs could not be distributed by rail. French intelligence agents reported locations of V-bomb depots and these were then heavily attacked.

The task of denying the enemy the use of railway communications was attempted by making marshalling yards the principal targets. Bennett found that these were not strongly defended; this gave the bomber crews a relative holiday from the intense reception to which they were accustomed in Germany. His technique was again to make considerable use of Oboe and master bombers on each raid. Generally the attacks were conducted at a fairly low level, as low as 1,000 feet when there was considerable cloud. The target areas with their workshops were destroyed and photographic reconnaissance showed that the initial German attempts to effect repairs were gradually abandoned. It was against one of these relatively easy targets that a master bomber, Squadron Leader Cranswick, was shot down and lost his life. Bennett believed that Cranswick had carried out more operations than any other pilot in the Command, about 143 raids. "When one appreciates that each such raid was generally as dangerous as a major battle on land or sea one gets something of the idea of the sacrifice made by some bomber crews . . . yet the public have never heard of him."

The Pathfinders were also given the task of attacking enemy radar posts and gun batteries defending the coast of northern Europe. The target area was extensive, spreading from North Holland to Ushant in western France, in order to avoid revealing to the Germans those areas where landings would eventually be attempted. The rule was that for every raid made against a target in the intended invasion area, three other targets outside that area had also to be attacked. Thus three-quarters of the effort was wasted in the interests of security.

Bennett was present at a pre-invasion conference of senior officers of the three services when the representative of the Royal Navy identified ten batteries of heavy guns in concrete emplacements covering the landing beaches. He explained that each of the guns could sink a landing craft with a single round if it scored a hit and that the conditions for accuracy would be relatively easy. He demanded a definite 100 per cent guarantee from Bomber Command that all of these guns would be put out of action before the landing craft came within their range. It was a tall order, and the senior RAF officer present looked at Bennett and said that it was up to him to declare whether the Pathfinders could accomplish what was asked.

The ten batteries were not to be attacked until six hours before the landings in order to keep the Germans guessing. Bennett did some rapid thinking and realised that in the worst possible case of solid fog merging into thick cloud continuously up to a very high level, no marking methods whatever could be used and it would be impossible to destroy the guns. Yet if such weather were prevailing it would be most unlikely that Eisenhower would give the word to go because of the problems which such conditions would pose for the marine craft. He replied to the naval representative that he could give a ninety-five per cent guarantee that he could destroy the guns if the weather was clear and could do so even if there were a layer of cloud or fog over them. He went on to explain his reasoning over the weather aspect. This seemed to satisfy the naval representative but left Bennett wondering whether they appreciated what an enormous responsibility he was being asked to accept, since there would be a huge number of casualties if the guns were not put out of action and the results might be catastrophic. He reflected that the very success of Pathfinder Force in the past had accustomed people to ask him to achieve things which they themselves had no idea of the means nor the method of doing.

In the weeks before D-Day, Pathfinder Force continued to attack railway installations, coastal radar, gun positions and V-bomb sites. When the weather over France was bad they were allowed to attack German targets, particularly those associated with the aircraft industry. It was a measure of the success of Bomber Command that the Germans had given top priority to the production of fighters and night fighters and were putting very little effort into the manufacture of bombers. This was going to prove extremely important when Allied forces landed again in Europe because there proved to be very few air attacks directed against them. Nor was Hitler able to mount any serious retaliatory assaults from the air against Britain.

Until a very late stage Bennett did not know the exact date when the invasion would take place, nor did he wish to know until he had to. He was certainly well aware of all the preparations: the assembly of great numbers and varieties of surface craft, the creation of Mulberry harbour and the production of the PLUTO pipeline by his scientist friends, who had developed Fido with such success. His anxieties about the weather and the guarantee he had given to the Navy about silencing the gun batteries were reinforced by the general lack of knowledge about the current strength of the German army in Europe.

The chosen D-Day was 5th June. The troops would have to be embarked on the previous day, when General Eisenhower and his senior commanders met early in the morning to make a decision. The forecasters were pessimistic; the Navy were against the operation and Leigh Mallory commanding the Tactical Air Force also voted for a postponement. This was a great relief to Bennett, who by now was sharing the burden of secrecy over the invasion date. Twenty-four hours later, a more favourable forecast was forthcoming, and this time the invasion was set in train. That night Bennett took part in the planning for bombing the beach areas. The full weight of Bomber Command was available, except for some Lancasters and other aircraft employed to distribute "Window" and give the impression of a movement of ships in a different part of the Channel. He disapproved of the diversion of valuable aircraft for such a purpose, which he believed could easily have been achieved by light marine craft, and maintained, "Being clever for cleverness' sake has never had much appeal to me." During the night, Pathfinders attacked various targets before attending to their main job only four hours before the invasion.

All ten of the vital aiming points were marked by Oboe; eight of these were controlled and marked by Pathfinders. The two remaining targets were controlled and marked by 83 and 97 Squadrons, which had been made the responsibility of 5 Group. These two targets were also bombed by 5 Group. There was broken cloud at various levels, but all the Pathfinders' markers were seen and excellent results were obtained. It was a triumph once again for Oboe, with very great credit going also to the master bombers. Bennett reported, "From all the eight targets marked and controlled by the Pathfinder Force I believe there was not a gun firing. Of the remaining two batteries 5 Group did a really good job on them, and with the exception, I believe, of one gun which was firing on manual control those batteries too were out of action."

In the tense and critical days that followed the invasion, the Germans fought hard and took a great deal of moving. Bomber Command was, at least in theory, not intended to be used for short term tactical purposes but the vast weight of bombs which it alone could put down was so powerful a weapon that General Montgomery could not resist the temptation to appeal for strikes against tactical targets. Bennett sent Mosquito bombers against targets in Germany, but Oboe Mosquitoes were used to mark eight targets on the night after the invasion. On the night of 7th June six more tactical targets were marked, and on both occasions Lancasters of his 8 Group did the bombing. On the night of the 8th and 9th June, Pathfinder Force returned to the attack on marshalling yards, but, as Bennett put it, "just to show the Germans that the invasion would not relieve them of their worries at home I sent three dozen Mosquitoes to Berlin. We carried on along these lines and gave local airfields which had fighters on them a good pounding every now and again just to help keep any air force animosity at bay, or at least suitably discouraged."

Both Bomber Command and the United States Air Force had been carrying out regular attacks on airfields west of the Rhine, while only Bennett's Mosquito bombers continued their assaults on Berlin, Cologne and other German cities, "to let the population know that Bomber Command would not forget them. Politically this was of tremendous importance and I am glad that we had those Mosquitoes available to do it— in spite of the bureaucrats." The value to the Army of Bomber Command was so speedily evident that by 12th June it was being asked to attack Caen itself right in front of the British troops. Harris was prompted to remark that his Bomber Command were being expected to invent "suction bombs" for the Army. First a vast tonnage of bombs would be dropped, and when the Army had advanced through the remaining dazed and stupefied German troops, they would stop again and demand another heavy load of bombs to be laid in front of them. He added, "The irony of it was that they then complained that we made the ground impossible to pass through with their vehicles."

For Bennett, whose aircraft were being employed in close tactical support of the troops, the problem was to avoid hitting them. Heavy bombers had never been used on any great scale for such a role. He was well aware that a crew could make a mistake and release bombs short of the target; that this could also happen as a consequence of an electrical fault in the bomb release circuit. On one of the first tactical raids, he flew himself to observe how things were going and was very relieved to see no stray bombs falling dangerously short of the target.

Early in August, what Bennett had feared came to pass. Attending a meeting at the Air Ministry, reports came in that Bomber Command aircraft had been bombing our own troops: "I was certainly put in a most difficult position by some of my seniors present . . . I feel they might at least have investigated the cause of the trouble before giving me quite such a hot time." In due course Bennett discovered that one aircraft had dropped its bombs short of the target when the route had, contrary to the wishes of Pathfinder Force, taken the bombers directly over Allied troops. The local Army officers let off smoke candles of a colour agreed with the Tactical Air Force to identify their men on that particular day, "but unfortunately," Bennett wrote, "our magnificent liaison had failed to convey this information to Bomber Command." It was doubly unfortunate that the colour the Army had used that day was that used by the Pathfinders for their aiming point. Some main force bombers saw the colour and bombed it although the majority realised that there had been a mistake and flew on to the correct target and the true aiming point. Sadly, the number of casualties among the ground forces was high and included many Canadians. Not only did Bomber Command not know that the Army had decided an identifying system with the Tactical Air Force, but Harris had made an arrangement that the Army would not use coloured smoke when Bomber Command was operating.

The German Panzer divisions were concentrating the weight of their armour against General Montgomery and the British troops in the northern sector of operations in France. The Americans were advancing on a broad front further south, and Bennett shared the impatience felt by many people in Britain at the time that the progress of the British and Canadian armies was all too slow. In a fit of exasperation at some example of poor liaison, Bennett went to see Montgomery's Chief of Staff, De Guingand. Not totally convinced that things were going more or less to the army commander's plan, Bennett tried to explain how keen both Bomber Command and Pathfinder Force were to be of assistance and how much they could offer. The existing machinery for liaison between the two services was quite unsuited to cope with the rapidly changing strategic situations; it was preposterous to allow a delay of two days to elapse before any large scale support from the RAF was forthcoming. Bennett told De Guingand that it was his personal view that in a real emergency Bomber Command would always come to the help of the Army and that Harris was keen to assist in every way. Stressing that it was his own opinion, Bennett suggested that Bomber Command should be able to put on a hundred heavy bombers at thirty minutes' notice.

Not long after this meeting Bennett was able to prove his point. The great bulk of the German armour and their main troop concentrations still opposed the British beyond Caen, whilst the Americans had broken through the German defences and were coming round in a left hand encircling movement. The Canadians were brought in on the British left and advanced towards Falaise. Close support was provided by Bomber Command to help in the decisive battle of the campaign. The Pathfinders marked numerous aiming points and gave valuable assistance to the Army. Then Bennett received a telephone call from Saundby, recently promoted to be deputy to Harris. The Army had discovered that the Germans were retreating towards Argentan and Gace down what was called the Falaise Gap, and this west to east road had to be blocked. It was impossible to take Bomber Command off the targets already allocated for that evening, but would it be possible for Bennett to mark that escape route and put on whatever aircraft could be brought into action at such short notice?

It was exactly the challenge Bennett welcomed. Over 100 heavy aircraft were sent in to the attack and the Pathfinders carried out completely blind marking in a place where the surrounding country made it impossible for wheeled vehicles to move off the road. "We ploughed up the whole area," he reported, "and brought the traffic to a complete standstill . . . it stopped the rat-run and thus bottled up the Germans in what became their slaughter-ground, a slaughter far greater than the people of England ever realised. The defeat . . . was probably the most serious of the whole war."

Not for the first time Bennett was irritated by the failure of the Army to acknowledge the help accorded to them: "Their operational research into the great success of that battle apparently overlooked this little raid entirely. It was again so when we interfered seriously with the enemy during the later Ardennes offensive by Rundstedt." A different raid in a different place provided an example of what Bennett called "the staunch loyalty of the British press to the Senior Service whenever possible." As the armies moved eastwards, various pockets of resistance remained to be dealt with. Le Havre was outflanked when the Allies crossed the Seine, and Bomber Commmand was called upon to attack gun emplacements around the port. Then one day about 1,000 heavy aircraft each carrying about six tons of bombs were brought in to reduce the enemy. To the north of Le Havre facing the English Channel were some gun emplacements, the sole purpose of which was to shoot out to sea. They were not an embarrassment to the Army, nor could they prevent any attack upon the town, but fifty heavy bombers were ordered to drop 300 tons of high explosive to silence the guns. The reason for this was to allow HMS *Erebus*, a gunboat of very ancient vintage, to come within range of Le Havre so that she too could join in the shelling. Bennett watched the action throughout its entire duration. He observed the waste of 300 tons of high explosive by the bombers on guns which threatened nobody, and he watched HMS *Erebus* firing for many hours a total of less than fifty tons of high explosive. "I am not belittling what *Erebus* did," he wrote, "but what I am saying is that the great British Press the next morning need not have carried banner headlines to say that the Royal Navy had shelled Le Havre and that the gunfire from Le Havre was heard in London, when in fact this action on the part of the Royal Navy was indeed a very minor one in relation to the might of Bomber Command."

As the summer and autumn of 1944 gave way to winter, Bomber Command's main weight often returned to the cities of Germany, particularly when the weather over the armies locked on the western front made it more profitable to attack industrial targets. In France, Bennett followed up the Allied forces with his Oboe stations, now produced for him by the boffins in a mobile form. More Oboe controllers and technical assistants had to be trained and vehicles provided to move them about. Oboe became effective deep into enemy territory within a few days of each movement forward of the Army and was essential for accuracy and reliability under all conditions; H₂S was at a disadvantage over open country where there were no built-up areas to differentiate on the screen. Bennett gave the scientists and signals experts "full marks for the wonderful way in which they met the occasion and produced the goods in time."

Once the Allied ground forces had crossed the Seine, the troops under Montgomery had to fight hard to capture the Channel ports, Brussels and Antwerp. Along with many others, Bennett assumed that their drive would go straight on through Holland into Germany and bring the war to a rapid conclusion. But not only did the Germans continue to fight with tremendous spirit, the Army was delayed by great difficulties with its supply lines. Bennett was perplexed that "even in a relatively modern war the whole of the forward troops depend on the roads and the roads alone for supplies. It is easy to see how inadequate these are even with thousands and thousands of lorries at the disposal of the Army when one realises the narrow strips which roads present on the surface of the earth. The vast spaces of the air were virtually unused." Bennett believed that the failure of either side to use the air to supply its forces was one of the great lessons of the war.

To speed up the advance, a plan was devised to drop airborne troops behind the enemy lines to capture and prevent the destruction of some of the canal bridges before the retreating Germans could destroy them. The important bridges were at Arnhem and Nijmegen. The troops were dropped on 17th September, and as the reports of events came in Bennett was sickened to find that the Dakotas had routed straight down a line of defences clearly shown in the intelligence records. Flown at 2,000 feet they were sitting ducks for the light flak. In the days which followed, the subsequent "drops" did not experiment with an improved route or tactics and the casualties were inordinately high. The heavy losses had an effect and there was intense German reaction around the bridges. Poor weather prevented air supplies reaching the beleaguered airborne troops and Bennett rang up Bomber Command HQ to suggest that he should make a blind drop of supplies as it was obvious that the ordinary visual methods adopted by the Army's tactical units were quite inadequate in the prevailing conditions. While he awaited some response, the weather deteriorated and reports from the bridgehead indicated that the operation was likely to prove a complete failure. Bennett telephoned again and pleaded with Saundby to be allowed to put down some supplies by aircraft equipped with Oboe. He wrote bitterly, "Still my suggestion reaped no reward. I don't know whether Bomber Command even offered our services to the Army, but whether they did or not it was a deplorable thing that we were not allowed to help." Bennett believed that supplies of anti-tank weapons and ammunition might have made all the difference, for the Germans had been able to deploy relatively few tanks against the airborne troops. "The gallantry of our troops", he wrote, "was magnificent. Their support from behind was dismal . . . the tactical planning of the initial drop was pathetic . . . The failure to hold this vital bridge was of tremendous importance in the termination of the war which in my view would have come to an end in a very short time had we been successful."

With the approach of winter, Bennett continued to send his Pathfinders to hammer German cities with occasional diversions for tactical purposes. It was clear to him that the Army was—in his own words— "getting ready for something big but of course we in the Air Force were not fully informed of those parts of the overall strategy which obviously had nothing to do with us." On 16th December, 1944, he had a telephone call from the senior Oboe controller of a unit sited beyond the Meuse up on one of the hills in the western portion of the Ardennes. He reported to Bennett that the Germans had launched a counter attack, forcing him to retire at all speed to avoid capture and that consequently the Oboe station was off the air. The controller insisted that the offensive was a major one and that the raw American troops who had only recently taken up position in the area "were collapsing like green cheese". Bennett telephoned to Bomber Command with this information, but they did not take the news very seriously.

It was the beginning of the Rundstedt offensive through the Ardennes, deliberately initiated when the weather was very bad because with relatively little air support available to back up their drive the Germans wanted to avoid harrassment from Allied tactical aircraft. It was obvious to Bennett that the enemy were trying to drive westward to recapture Liège and Brussels and the port of Antwerp, thereby cutting off supplies to the British and American armies. Montgomery reacted very swiftly, bringing troops to hold the spearhead of the German offensive, and Bomber Command laid on eight major raids in which Pathfinder Force played an important part. The fog over England, Belgium and the battle area was in general very thick, but at Graveley and at Downham Market Fido was available to land back those aircraft which were sent out on raids. In every case blind marking was necessary, because even in daylight the ground was not visible. The most vitally important raid in the opinion of Bennett was against the St Vith crossroads, which was in the heart of the Ardennes mountains with roads converging towards it from all directions. Any traffic moving between east and west had to pass through St Vith; it was thus of supreme importance in supplying the Germans spearhead. The crossroads was blanketed by thick fog, but it was marked by Target Indicators and so efficiently bombed that supplies to the German spearhead dried up. The German tank crews were denied fuel to continue and had to dig themselves in and fight with what remained of their ammunition.

Some time after the defeat of the Ardennes offensive, Bennett was stung by remarks that Rundstedt's drive was doomed to failure from the outset. In his opinion the situation at the time was extremely serious; he gave full credit to the tactics employed by Montgomery and added, "It would have been difficult to hold the Germans' offensive . . . had they not been short of supplies brought about first in a general sense by the effect of Bomber Command's bombing of Germany, particularly at that time of their synthetic fuel supplies and secondly by the direct result of our own attacks upon them . . . This heavy support of the Army . . . was one of the things which I believe was seldom appreciated, particularly the vital effect of the St Vith raid."

The Pathfinders gave considerable assistance to the Allied armies fighting to recover the ground lost during the Ardennes offensive. Bennett and his staff selected a large number of railway tunnels in the hilly district immediately behind the German front and the Mosquito crews were ordered to approach these at a low level and drop their bombs into the tunnel mouths. Each bomb had a delayed-action fuse. Fifteen tunnels were skip-bombed in this way and most of these attacks caused some paralysis to the railway services in the district. One squadron was allocated this task on any one day, a remarkably economical exercise in terms of results.

Early in 1945, the crews of Pathfinder Force were assigned a novel task, that of dropping food supplies to the Dutch population, which had been suffering great privations whilst their country became a battlefield. But with the strength of Bomber Command at its peak Bennett was able to send several dozen Mosquitoes to bomb Berlin and follow up with three dozen Mosquitoes several hours later; others were sent over a whole range of German cities to keep the sirens wailing. In February, Oboe Mosquitoes carried out 427 operations, the Lancasters 866. Bennett's Mosquito bombers of what he liked to call the Light Night Striking Force carried out 1,809 operations during the month. Thus the total for 8 Group was 3,102 operations for the loss of only seventeen aircraft.

As the range of targets widened to include Czechoslovakia and eastern Germany, Harris suddenly made attacks on oil installations a priority target. Bennett could not at first understand this because hitherto the Commander in Chief had opposed such targets because of their difficult nature. When Harris eventually explained how critical Germany's oil situation was believed to be, he realised that the objective was a worthy one at that stage of the war. The synthetic plants in the Ruhr were given a good pounding, and

Bennett accepted that "we brought Germany to her knees more by this 'panacea' than by anything else in the closing stages of the war."

As the end drew near, Bomber Command reverted to a task it had been given in 1939—leaflet dropping. This time the intended recipients were not the Germans but their prisoners of war in camps still beyond the reach of the Allied armies. The object was to explain to them the military situation as it existed and give instructions as to behaviour and the procedure which would be followed to protect and recover them as soon as possible.

Between 18th August, 1942, and 8th May, 1945, the aircraft under Bennett's command had flown 50,490 bombing sorties and attacked 3,440 targets. The casualties amounted to 3,618 men. Within Bomber Command as a whole about 55,000 members of air crews lost their lives. This compares with the loss during the first world war of 39,000 army officers, for the most part young subalterns on the western front. In Bennett's own words, "The contribution of an aircrew member of Bomber Command who completed an operational tour or died in the process, measured in terms of danger and death, both in intensity and duration, was in my view far greater than of any other fighting man, RAF, Navy or Army. The contribution of a Pathfinder, in the same terms of intensity and duration of danger—and indeed of responsibility, was at least twice that of other Bomber Command crews. Great Britain and the Empire have strangely failed to erect any Nelson's column in memory of Bomber Command, the most powerful striking force in all British history."

In the years that have passed since May 1945 it has become fashionable to regard the strategic bombing programme undertaken during the war as a costly failure. In 1965 A. J. P. Taylor wrote, "By early 1945 . . . the strategic air offensive belatedly achieved decisive results. This was mainly the work of the Americans." This conclusion is in plain contradiction of the facts. Certainly after 1942 Bomber Command made the decisive contribution to the successful conclusion of the war, and Harris carried a greater burden of responsibility than any other British commander. Others committed their forces at intervals, whereas night after night Harris sent out almost the whole of his command and on his shoulders rested the responsibility for Bomber Command's casualties. It was for him to decide the most effective and least wasteful way to operate the force he had built up. Under his command, Bennett's keenness and drive, his enormous capacity for work and his disdain for those who took refuge in the "official channels" must have made him at times an awkward subordinate to handle. Yet each had the highest regard for the other's professional qualities. Of Bennett the Commander in Chief wrote,

"His consciousness of his own intellectual powers sometimes made him impatient with slower or differently constituted minds so that some people found him difficult to work with. He could not suffer fools gladly and by his own high standards there were many fools . . . Being still a young man he underrated experience and over-rated knowledge, a young intellectual's habit . . . we were lucky to get a man of such attainments." When Harris had been ordered by Portal to set up a target finding force he had promised Bennett that he would offer him his personal support in every way. The latter confirmed that "This assurance was carried out to the letter and in the spirit from then on to the end of the war. He never really gave the Pathfinders a fair chance relative to other special units but he always supported me personally to the best of his ability and did everything he could to help me." The reservation implied in Bennett's remarks was a reference to the support given by Harris to Cochrane's independent actions against precise targets. The Commander in Chief must have been very well aware of the Pathfinder's antipathy to 5 Group's commander but he retained a high regard for his abilities. "An absolutely outstanding commander", he declared. "His group has been twice as effective as any other group in the Command . . . Cochrane is a genius . . . I always hoped that Cochrane would replace me here."

At the Telecommunication Research Centre a week after VE Day Bernard Lovell made an entry in his diary: "8 Group is scarcely any more and the Air Vice Marshal who caused us so much trouble but who was nevertheless one of our staunchest friends has grown into an MP. So that is that, and may the next scrap book be about electrons, neutrons and professors and not about scanners, cathode ray tubes and Air Marshals."

At the conclusion of the First World War the coalition government under Lloyd George had followed the traditional practice of paying substantial sums to leading commanders and staff officers. This had left a sour taste in the mouths of a great number of demobilised volunteers and conscripts, many of whom soon found themselves in the dole queues. The Labour Party won the general election of 1945 and there was to be no question of money payments and only a limited number of peerages. The absence of a peerage for Harris was conspicuous at the time and was widely regarded as a slight on Bomber Command. Nor was any campaign medal awarded to the air crew members of the command. Air Vice Marshal Bennett had been awarded the DSO for gallantry in 1942, when he escaped after bombing the *Tirpitz*, the CBE in 1943 and the CB in 1944, but he remained the only group commander without a knighthood at the conclusion of the war. Many regarded him as the architect of Bomber Command's efficiency and thus its ability to destroy the German Reich.

British South American Airways 9

BEFORE THE WAR had ended, even before the Allied invasion of Europe in 1944, the choice of Bennett as the man to assume operational control of the first British airline to fly to South America had entered someone's mind. This idea was conceived by John Booth, chairman of the General Council of British Shipping, on his travels in South America during the war. Convinced that it would be possible to operate an airline both economically and on a commercial basis, he found interested backers among those shipping companies already engaged in trade to the South American continent. In addition to his own Booth Steamship company, the Royal Mail Lines, Blue Star Line, Pacific Steam Navigation Company and Lamport and Holt Line all agreed to give financial support. Booth had an opportunity to introduce Bennett to nominees of these concerns in January, 1944, after which it was decided to offer him the post of operational director of their proposed company which would be called British Latin American Airlines. Meanwhile, as Bennett reminded the directors, the war had still to be won.

During 1945, Bennett let it be known that he had political ambitions, and all three of the political parties were eager to recruit him. However it was as a Liberal that he was induced to stand. With the support of the Secretary of State for Air, Sir Archibald Sinclair, who was also the leader of the Liberal party, Bennett was adopted as the candidate for election to the vacant seat of Middlesbrough West. His election was in fact a formality, under the wartime arrangement among the partners in the coalition government that the party of the previous sitting member would not have their candidate opposed. The German surrender in May, 1945, and the release of Bennett from the RAF meant that he was free to begin to organise the new airline. As the only director with any background in aviation it was inevitable that he shoud be given a free hand, and the shape of the company reflected his views.

It should have been possible, if the British Government had been asked to make the dollars available, to buy a number of surplus Douglas DC4 Skymasters, a type that had entered service in 1939 and was to be the principal flag carrier of many of the world's international carriers even after pressurised aircraft became available. By 1945 the Lockheed Constellation, which was pressurised, had also gone into production. It will be recalled, however, that Bennett had been offended at the merger of his previous employer Imperial Airways with a company that operated foreign machines, and there was no intention on his part to make use of anything other than British aircraft and equipment. A. V. Roe's Lancaster, which had performed so successfully as a bomber, could be converted into a transport aircraft capable of carrying thirteen passengers. It did not have a pressurised cabin, but an oxygen supply with tubes for passengers to suck could be provided for flights above 10,000 feet. The Avro York, with a more commodious cabin to accommodate twenty-one passengers, was also in production, but there was no provision of oxygen and this limited the operating ceiling. Powered by the same Rolls Royce Merlin engines as the Lancaster, it had a high noise level, while the fuselage, which could be described with fair accuracy as shaped like a brick rounded off at the edges, reduced the airspeed below that of the civil Lancastrian and degraded its performance. These two aircraft were of course stop-gaps until A. V. Roe had developed their new civil airliner, to be known as the Tudor.

Bennett faced the task of hiring pilots, wireless operators and other categories of staff. The enormous expansion of the RAF during the war may have resulted in a huge supply of men trained for specific duties in aviation, but the civil regulations required airline crews to hold licences. Those already possessing such qualifications had little difficulty obtaining appointments in BOAC

Avro Tudor IV of BSAA, 1948. Bennett family

and other existing companies. In the event, Bennett engaged only a few experienced airline personnel. One of these was Captain Gordon Store, who was appointed Operations Manager. It will be recalled that he and Bennett had both taken part in the flight refuelling trials of the flying boats on the trans-Atlantic flights in 1939 and subsequently assisted in the delivery of Hudsons to Britain from Gander. The Chief Pilot's office went to David Brice, who had also ferried Hudsons. These two men were the only former Imperial Airways pilots. For the most part Bennett recruited the men on whom he had relied in Pathfinder Force; fifteen pilots, mainly wing commanders who had distinguished themselves as master bombers, were engaged and at once began to study for the necessary civil licences. For Bennett, these licences had to include not only the civil pilot's B licence, which would be endorsed for the type of aircraft in which the individual had passed the technical examination, but also the First Class Navigator's licence, an essential pre-requisite for the trans-oceanic sectors that the airline would be flying. Bennett had no intention of employing non-pilot navigators except for a couple whom he engaged to instruct his pilots. The Radio Superintendent's job went to McGillivray, formerly of Imperial Airways, who was able to hire some qualified air operators, but some time had to pass before ex-RAF wireless operators could be trained up to international civil operating standards.

Bennett brought Pathfinder Force's most senior engineering officer into the airline to perform roughly his former function, but flight engineers were not required. As local managers at stations overseas, the men chosen were almost exclusively demobilised RAF officers, several of them Spanish speaking with experience as Air Attachés. Another had been the intelligence officer of Pathfinder Force, and the chief medical officer was also appointed to BSAA. The headquarters of the airline were in Grafton Street, near Piccadilly. It was Bennett's custom to interview even the most junior employees upon appointment, and a young apprentice to the traffic department recalls the lecture that he was given. Behind the director's desk was a large board with Bennett's name at the top. The interview satisfactorily concluded, Bennett had almost to kneel to add the youth's name at the base of the board. Forty years later and still in the airline business, Keith Hayward recalls the bustle in the building. Most of the staff still wore RAF uniform and office doors bore RAF ranks and the decorations of the occupant; maps and charts were spread everywhere. Down in the basement of the building was a canteen, which was shared with the employees of the adjoining hairdressing salon. Not sparing the time to go out and enjoy his lunch in more elegant surroundings, Bennett also patronised the canteen. The newspapers became interested in the

Proving flight to Buenos Aires in February, 1946. Left to Right: Captain Store, N/O Macilwaine, Captain MacMillan, Stargirl, Captain Brice and Captain Fordham.

new venture and featured accounts under such headlines as "Wing Commanders on probation". These stories provoked a member of parliament to put down a question in the House of Commons about the preponderance of former Pathfinder Force men in the new airline.

The general election which followed the German surrender obliged Bennett to defend his recently won seat. In the prevailing mood of the country, as peace returned, the seat was one of those captured by the Labour Party, and although this gave Bennett more time to devote to the airline, the change of government brought its problems. Not only had a Ministry of Civil aviation been created but it had been decided to split BOAC in order to establish another corporation to be responsible for air services within Europe. Furthermore, a team was to be sent to survey the route to South America, for the introduction of air services to that continent. Ominously for BLAA, the team were to travel in an aircraft flown by BOAC, and a request by the board of the newly formed company that their distinguished Chief Executive should be permitted to participate in the survey met with a refusal by the Ministry of Civil Aviation.

The Minister was Lord Winster. It fell upon Bennett to point out to him how much work had already been underaken to initiate the services and how much delay would ensue if the routes were allocated to BOAC. The new government then agreed that BLAA should be permitted to operate as a nationalised concern and take the name British South American Airways Corporation. Booth remained as Chairman and Bennett as Chief Executive. In November, 1945, when the House of Lords debated civil aviation, the former Chairman of BOAC, now Lord Reith, took part. He regretted the splitting up of the "chosen instrument" into three corporations with the consequent triplication of overheads and inevitable overlapping. He also foresaw the interference by government that was all too swiftly to infuriate Bennett. "It was soon obvious", Reith wrote, "that practically everything the air corporations did was to be shadowed by civil servants. Most shocking of all they were not to be allowed to order their own aircraft."

BOAC had expanded considerably during the war, using seconded RAF flight crews. The Air Ministry had made the RAF station at Ossington available to the senior corporation so that pilots, navigators and wireless operators could be given the instruction necessary for them to acquire the skills demanded of holders of civil licences. This facility was also offered to Bennett by one Group Captain Wilson, who was about to retire from his position in BOAC. "May I entreat you", he wrote, "not to allow the standards of qualification for commercial civil aviation aircrew to be lowered. On the contrary they should be made more comprehensive." In his reply Bennett declined the offer, writing, "I would stress that our requirements are higher than those of BOAC, not lower . . . our crews will come direct to us and undergo a short course in this company before starting the survey flights. Subsequently we would have our little training scheme working."

In view of what was to happen later, the qualifications demanded of pilots and particularly of navigators need to be appreciated. When Bennett wrote that his requirements were higher than those of BOAC he was referring specifically to the decision he had taken that all his pilots would be required to obtain a First Class Navigator's Licence. He did not intend non-pilot navigators to form part of his crews, but at that time it was permissible for a captain who possessed this qualification to transfer his attention to the navigation after take-off and resume his seat at the controls for the landing. In order to commence flights to South America as soon as possible, it was unavoidable that co-pilots should be hired who not only possessed no navigational qualifications but whose B licences were sometimes endorsed for an aircraft type other than a York or a Lancastrian. Bennett placed every such pilot under contract to pass the examination for a navigator's licence within three months, mainly by self-instruction, while the endorsement of his pilot's licence could be obtained by performing six landings on both the Lancastrian and the York in daylight to the satisfaction of a captain delegated by the company to supervise him. The availability of aircraft which were required neither for a scheduled service nor for routine maintenance in the hangar sometimes delayed this very necessary practice, and very few captains were sufficiently confident of their co-pilot's abilities to allow them to carry out landings on passenger services in the first year or more of the Company's operations.

Heathrow Airport was in the early process of construction throughout 1945. There was one completed runway but no hangars, and caravans, tents and pre-fabricated huts were sited adjacent to Bath Road. Bennett negotiated engineering facilities with Hawkers at their factory airfield a few miles away at Langley, and as each aircraft was delivered it was given a name which included the prefix "Star". The Company call sign was "Starline" and an emblem painted on the nose represented a Starman. On 1st January, 1946, he was in command of the Lancastrian *Star Light*, on the first commercial flight out of Heathrow and the first of a British airline to Argentina. The Minister of Civil Aviation, Lord Winster, was present to make an address appropriate to the occasion, after which Bennett, dressed in black Homburg hat and converted RAF greatcoat, led his crew on board. These included the airline's one and only stewardess, who was a former Air Transport Auxiliary Pilot, and two ground engineers to look after the aircraft at transit stops. The passengers who were carried were the men chosen to represent the airline at stations overseas. One of Bennett's rules for his staff was that they should not only abstain from alchoholic refreshment when in uniform, a sensible requirement, but also from smoking. Safety regulations at the time banned smoking in many British aircraft but the smokers among flight crews would have welcomed the opportunity to enjoy a cigarette or pipe in the airport building during transit stops. Bennett himself neither smoked nor drank anything containing alcohol.

The route to Buenos Aires was via Lisbon, Bathurst (now called Banjul), Natal, Rio de Janeiro and Montevideo. In Rio de Janeiro considerable interest had been aroused at the expected arrival of a British four engined airliner. The existing Santos Dumont Airport alongside the city and adjoining the bay possessed only one runway, whose length was really only adequate for the smaller twin engined Douglas DC3, which was then the principal flag carrier of the South American airlines. However, Bennett impressed the Brazilians with a perfect landing comfortably within the runway length.

By mid-March, further Lancastrians had been delivered to BSAA and a twice weekly service to Buenos Aires inaugurated. The following month a survey flight was conducted to Santiago: a Lancastrian crossed the Andes at 25,000 feet. This was a notable event because without exception all the existing air carriers had been obliged to fly this sector in almost clear weather. The Andes passage involved flying through valleys at about 13,000 feet in conditions often turbulent, an alarming experience for nervous passengers gazing out at the Andes peaks towering above them on either side. The highest of these was Mount Aconcagua, rising to over 23,000 feet above sea level. From Santiago, the survey flight continued to Peru, Columbia and Venezuela.

During the summer of 1946, Bennett conducted further flights to the Caribbean via Lisbon and the Azores. When enough Yorks had been delivered, this type of aircraft was used exclusively on the east coast service to South America, while the Lancastrian was operated across the Atlantic to Bermuda and thence via

Lord Winster, Minister for Civil Aviation, at the microphone when Star Light *made the first flight from Heathrow. Air Vice Marshal Bennett (with brief case) stands next to Captain Cracknell.* BBC Hulton Picture Library

113

Nassau, Jamaica, Venezuela and Peru to Chile and Argentina. The crews flew on both types of aircraft. Until the mid-Atlantic service to the Caribbean was opened, the longest sector flown was between West Africa and Natal in northern Brazil. Although what is known as the intertropical zone lies across this track and thunderstorms can be expected, the winds at the usual operating height of 10,000 feet are seldom strong; consequently navigation was not difficult. There were so few aircraft flying the route that there was little in the way of air traffic control and captains could choose flight levels and tracks to achieve the best time and to avoid the worst of the weather. However, in the vicinity of the airports there was control, and here the lack of a radio compass on the company's aircraft instrument panel made it impracticable for pilots to conform to the standard racetrack-shaped holding pattern above a radio beacon while waiting for permission to descend. At that time no British firm manufactured a radio compass.

After his inaugural flight to Santos Dumont, Bennett had obtained permission from the Brazilian authorities for his company's aircraft to use the new airport under construction on Governor's Island in the bay. The airline was also allowed to carry out the only type of holding pattern possible with their RAF type radio receiver, a box-shaped pattern. Some captains, however, preferred to save time by descending over the ocean until they were beneath the lowest layer of cloud and then to fly through the harbour mouth and past the famous "sugar loaf mountain" towards the airfield. On at least one occasion the masts of a ship were barely cleared.

Bennett's policy of using only British made equipment was accompanied by a determination that BSAA should operate at a profit, and the staff were expected to apply themselves to a variety of tasks. A senior member of management would find himself clutching a tripod in the middle of London Airport, helping the duty flight crew to adjust the compasses of an aircraft, on a Sunday morning when he had looked forward to a game of golf. A duty crew was rostered every day for such chores, to ferry aircraft to and from Langley and to carry out air tests on machines before a service departure. Bennett set an example, on more than one occasion taking off in a Lancastrian from Langley's grass field at night, when the sodden ground had frozen, his only illumination provided by the aircraft's landing lights.

It may be that the transformation to civil airline flying was not expected to present many difficulties, that too much confidence was placed on pilots who had braved anti-aircraft fire and night fighters in the recent past. In September, 1946, a York took off from Bathurst to make the journey across the South Atlantic to Brazil. Moments later it crashed, killing all on board, in the airline's first fatal accident. The weight of the aircraft on take-off was within the legal limits, but in those days no allowance was made for the effect of temperature on aircraft performance. It could not be determined whether an outboard engine had failed at a critical stage during the take-off, but if it had, it is doubtful whether in the prevailing steamy temperature conditions a positive rate of climb could have been achieved. The report of the Board of Enquiry disclosed that the captain was on his first trip in command of a York, having flown on one trip as a co-pilot; he had never had to perform a take-off in a York at that weight and temperature, and the co-pilot's licence was not endorsed for any four engined aircraft. The investigators concluded that for reasons unknown, but possibly connected with the pilot's inexperience, the controls had been mishandled. No regulations had been broken. In the early years after the war other operators were functioning in much the same way.

There was no shortage of passengers. Losses of shipping had created a huge backlog of applications for a seat on an aircraft or a berth on a ship, and BSAA was the first airline to restore links between Europe and South America. Indeed, government agencies intervened in seat allocation and demanded a priority for their nominees ahead of ordinary passengers.

The use of the new international airport on Governor's Island in the bay of Rio de Janeiro necessitated the employment of a launch to ferry the local staff and customs officials to meet the passengers, as there was no bridge linking the island to the mainland. This presented a splendid opportunity for the ferry operators to take advantage of their monopoly and to exact a heavy toll from users. It was a challenge that Bennett chose to take up. As no suitable vessel could be bought in Rio he purchased a surplus motor torpedo boat from the Admiralty and with his wife and a crew of volunteers embarked on the craft at Tower Wharf. He set off from the Thames estuary with great enthusiasm, but both engines performed badly due to a fuel feed problem, and Bennett put into Dover. One week before Christmas, 1946, assured that the problem would not recur, they departed once again en route to Lisbon. The trouble did recur and a diversion was made into the small French harbour of Ouessant. Deciding that it would be foolhardy to attempt the ocean crossing, Bennett set course for home, undertaking the loathsome task of sucking petrol out of the fuel tank with a hose pipe into a bucket and then pouring it down an open-ended pipe into the engine. Surprisingly, he insists that he alone among the crew was not sea-sick. Only later did he learn that the Royal Navy always modified the fuel system before putting to sea. Bennett sold it and continued to hire water transport in Rio harbour until the bridge to the airport was finally built.

In February, 1947, BSAA obtained a charter to fly a plane load of Greek seamen to join a ship in New Zealand. There was an epidemic of influenza at the time and Gordon Store told Bennett that he could muster neither a captain nor a stewardess without interfering with the crew roster for scheduled services. This was out of the question, so although Bennett had an important engagement to fulfil in the near future, he decided to fly out the seamen in a York himself and to complete the whole journey in as short a time as possible. With a co-pilot, two radio officers and two stewardesses he planned to conduct the flight with crew members taking it in turn to sleep on board and with stops en route only for fuel and essential servicing. Bennett's wife and his secretary both agreed to perform the role of stewardesses. Neither had any experience, but it was customary in BSAA for "stargirls", as they were called, to learn how to do the job in the course of passenger flights.

From London Airport they flew to Athens, where the seamen embarked, then it was on to Cairo and Karachi, where owing to a problem over the seamen's yellow fever inoculations, four hours' sleep on the ground was obtained by the air crew. When the flight was resumed, landings were made at Calcutta, Singapore, Darwin, Sydney and the destination airfield in New Zealand. The following day the York was flown to Brisbane, Bennett's home town, where the crew attended a reception in his honour. Then it was back to England without any stopovers for rest on the ground.

For the man who had flown *Mercury* to Montreal with one companion, a wireless operator, in twenty hours and then continued to New York after refuelling, this return flight with a co-pilot and two radio officers cannot have seemed an exceptional feat. The actual flying hours logged did not exceed those permitted by the regulations, which specified only a total not to be exceeded during thirty days; there was no legislation limiting continuous hours on duty. Airline managements drew up schedules and a captain was entitled to use his discretion when to continue or to halt his flight. This left enormous latitude to those who planned the crew schedules because captains felt under an obligation to attempt to abide by them, and some years passed before the authorities made a serious effort to control the situation. Meanwhile airline managements frequently sent letters of appreciation to crews who overcame schedule disruption through weather or servicing delays by extended spells of flying. In the enthusiastic and loyal atmosphere among the pilots of BSAA so soon after the airline's inauguration there was an eagerness to help out in this way.

In April, another accident to a BSAA York highlighted a different problem for the airline. After the disaster at Bathurst it had been decided to make Dakar in Senegal the African staging post for the South Atlantic crossing. About ninety miles to the north of Bathurst, this area is affected by monsoon rains for only four months of the year as against eight months at the former airport. The runway surface was also superior, but poor visibility and the lack of either approach lighting or a radio beacon contributed to this second accident.

The York approaching Dakar that night had made a normal transit of Lisbon on the way south from London. Shortly before the captain began his descent towards the airfield he conversed with the pilot of the north bound company aircraft, who mentioned that he had noticed patches of mist forming at the time of his departure. There was no radio facility available at Dakar for a pilot to carry out an instrument approach, and the powerful beams of a lighthouse on the coast near the airport were no use to a pilot who could not see the runway lights soon enough to be able to line up his aircraft for an approach. The York had enough fuel for a diversion to Bathurst but the decision to divert would have had to be taken without delay. After the captain had made two unsuccessful attempts to find the runway, the airport controller suggested a diversion to a nearby airfield called Thies. The crew possessed no chart for Thies and in any case the controller had no means of communicating with his colleague there, nor was its runway lit. Forced to attempt a landing before his fuel ran out, the pilot overshot the runway and some passengers were killed as the aircraft struck trees before coming to a stop.

Bennett flew out to Dakar at once to carry out a personal investigation, after issuing a statement that fog was almost unknown in Dakar. Sadly, however, the lack of adequate facilities for an instrument approach was commonplace at innumerable airfields in use throughout the world. Runway and approach lighting was also inadequate, although wartime pilots were accustomed to a minimum standard that did not attract enemy bombers or intruders. Even at London Airport, the illumination of the Bath Road was brighter than that provided for the runway running parallel to it.

The Lancastrians remained in service, operating to Santiago via Lisbon, the Azores, Bermuda, Jamaica, Colombia and Peru. The York did not possess the range to operate between the Azores and Bermuda, a distance of 2,260 nautical miles and the longest ocean sector operated by any airline during the 1940s. The airfield at Santa Maria on the Azores served only as a refuelling stop, passengers neither joining there nor disembarking. Trials were undertaken to test the possibility of refuelling the aircraft in flight on the way from London to Bermuda. An aircraft operated by Sir Alan Cobham's company, Flight Refuelling, based in the Azores, would fly to a point about 300 miles to the north of the islands,

Sir Alan Cobham and Air Vice Marshal Bennett departing on the non-stop Lancastrian flight to Bermuda.
Bennett family

where it would make contact with the Lancastrian and replenish the airliner's tanks. True to form, Bennett commanded the first trial himself, and Sir Alan Cobham joined the crew to observe proceedings. One of his own company engineers was also on board to handle the hoses from the tanker aircraft. On each aircraft the radio officers watched their cathode ray tubes and particularly the small pulse which identified the approaching machine. The tanker positioned itself overhead, extended the hose and 2,000 gallons were transferred. There remained the long journey to Bermuda, and four bunks had been fitted to allow those on board an opportunity to sleep. During the night a problem arose: in the process of transferring fuel from the extra tank to the wing tanks all four generators had burnt out. Everything electrical was switched off to save the aircraft accumulators for driving the transfer pump to complete the fuel transfer, which soon resulted in a dead flat battery. Bennett attempted to navigate by the stars, but they were often obscured by a cover of high cloud and the flight continued with all on board hoping that the forecast winds were correct and that the aircraft would arrive near enough to Bermuda for the island to be visible. At the estimated time of arrival no island was seen, just night and a black sea. Some time went by before the first officer saw the light from the Cooks Point light house.

A number of these return flights were made thereafter, and all the others passed off successfully without any untoward incident. The distance of 3,355 nautical miles was usually flown in about 20 hours. The Ministry of Civil Aviation had sponsored the trials in anticipation of the forthcoming introduction of A. V. Roe's new pressurised Tudor airliner, which had been ordered by Bennett to replace the Lancastrians. It was intended that the Tudor should also go into service with BOAC but it had become apparent that the senior corporation was anything but enthusiastic about it. The other major airlines, particularly those that had bought the Lockheed Constellations, seemed to offer competition far too strong for the Tudor, which in the lay-out envisaged by BOAC for the North Atlantic route would be able to carry only twelve passengers while requiring a crew of six. A committee that investigated BOAC's final rejection admitted that the aircraft possessed some undesirable characteristics but maintained that the basic design was sound. Bennett was in no way influenced by BOAC's decision and in August, 1947, he flew a Tudor to Jamaica for tropical trials. A week was spent in the Caribbean, after which he declared himself satisfied with the aircraft's performance and stated that no modifications were required. The Air Registration Board expressed approval and arrangements were made to take delivery of the version known as the Tudor IV. There would be no provision for a flight engineer, so the officer navigating would have near his desk the controls for the heating and pressurisation system. With a radio officer and two stewardesses the crew would number six but the American radio equipment fitted in the rejected BOAC version would be removed and the standard RAF receivers and transmitters put in their place. The aircraft cabin would accommodate 32 passengers.

Before the first Tudor was delivered, however, another disaster struck the company. A Lancastrian was en route from Buenos Aires to Santiago, on a day when bad weather over the Andes had grounded all the other carriers, who never attempted to make the crossing unless the passage through the valleys could be completed visually. Bennett had also forbidden his captains to fly over the Andes unless they could do so without entering cloud. The Lancastrian *Star Dust* was being flown by a pilot on his first command. No one knows what happened, because the aircraft wreckage was never found, but repeated requests from ground stations for a position report brought the reply "Stand by". It is probable that the pilot was trying to find a way to make the crossing in visual conditions, and the most likely assumption is that he could not avoid the rising cumulus storm clouds, the aircraft becoming unstable as ice covered the wings.

Bennett set off for South America with the intention of conducting his own search in the Lancastrian freighter that was based in Montevideo for the movement of spare engines and equipment. On the way, sitting in the passenger cabin of a York, he was called upon by the captain to clear a snag to the aircraft's radio receiver which had stumped the embarrassed radio officer. He went forward, swiftly analysed the problem, rectified the fault and returned to his seat.

On his arrival in Buenos Aires, he found that both the Argentine and Chilean authorities who had initially set in train an air search for the Lancastrian had already abandoned their attempts, convinced that no one could have survived the bitter conditions prevailing among the Andes mountains in winter. Undaunted, he mustered a BSAA crew and a few of the local staff as extra pairs of eyes and flew towards Mendoza at the foothills of the Andes. Before landing, he piloted the Lancastrian through valleys and along the sides of the peaks while everyone on board stared out, uneasily aware that never before had they flown so close to rising ground of such awesome proportions. Bennett landed before night-fall and resumed the quest at first light, having arranged for supplies to be packed in bright red containers which would show up against the snow if the aircraft wreckage was observed. But, after several days' searching without any clues to the likely area of impact Bennett flew back to Buenos Aires and accompanied the search crew on their return to England.

The following month, September, 1947, must have seemed to herald a more auspicious future for the young and very enthusiastic company. At Woodford, the works airfield of A. V. Roe, the first of BSAA's Tudor IVs was ready for delivery. Bennett took a crew to collect it and had already fixed the following day for the departure of a proving and goodwill flight, which unusually on such occasions would include the carriage of paying passengers. At Woodford the technical formalities involved a delay that prevented Bennett taking off in daylight. There were no night flying facilities at Woodford but by the light of the moon, the headlights of cars and the aircraft's own landing lights Bennett took off for London Airport.

The journey of the Tudor through the airline's growing network in South America and the Caribbean culminated in a further statement from Bennett that from the point of view of comfort, noise level, payload and cost of operation, the Tudor was ten per cent better than the Constellation and equal in speed. It was also, he said, "The most silent aircraft I have ever experienced." Always optimistic, Bennett had been most anxious for BSAA to show a profit in the first year of operation, and this was achieved.

Passengers boarding BSAA Tudor IV, 1948.
British Airways

He did not conceal his opinion that BOAC was grossly over-staffed and generally inefficient, and this view gained adherents from among those who observed the proliferation of "stop-gap" aircraft such as Haltons, derived from the Halifax bomber, and the continuation of the increasingly uneconomic flying boat services. Most of the world's major airlines had rejected these and planned to introduce larger, faster, more economical airliners able to fly above the worst of the weather.

If the Tudor was to prove as good as Bennett proclaimed, then the outlook for BSAA was bright. He was the chief propagandist for this airliner and for the next few years would continue to defend it against its critics. Meanwhile, the plan was that all the Lancastrians and Yorks, already facing competition from the Skymasters of Air France and KLM, would be phased out as deliveries of Tudors took place. The airline's route structure was extended by the acquisition of a controlling interest in British West Indian Airways in order that this company's twin engined machines, which served the small airports of the islands, could complement the services offered to long distance passengers. It was typical of Bennett, when replying to the enquiry of his local manager whether he might retain members of BWIA's ground staff, to issue a rebuke for "the sort of letter one might expect from an executive of BOAC."

The pilots of BSAA, required to make themselves proficient navigators, had taken up the challenge with zest and were disappointed on those occasions when St Paul's Rocks, a tiny outcrop on the direct track between Africa and Brazil, had been overflown unobserved. Much more formidable, however, was the burden on the navigator responsible for the sector from the Azores to Bermuda. There was little in the way of shipping plying the ocean at this latitude, so radio bearings could seldom be obtained. There were no ocean station vessels—weather ships—as were available on the North Atlantic route. The knowledge of upper wind strength and direction over this huge stretch of water was minimal and it soon became apparent that the forecast by the meteorology office in the Azores was dangerously misleading. Moreover, there was no alternative airport available to the pilot on the westerly track if due to weather or other cause a landing could not be made at Bermuda; a decision to divert to Gander had to be made at a comparatively early stage in the flight. Consequently, pilots were instructed to carry fuel for ninety minutes' flying in addition to the total estimated as necessary for the flight between the two airports. Fog and low cloud are extremely rare at Bermuda, but heavy rain and strong winds are not uncommon. There had already been one occasion when a Lancastrian had arrived over the airport while the island was suffering its worst storm in 50 years. The aircraft had been severely damaged when the pilot had to attempt a landing on the flooded airfield.

The Tudor was equipped to carry 32 passengers in a heated and pressurised cabin at altitudes above 20,000 feet, but as with most new ventures it had its snags. The heating system was unreliable, and when it failed captains had no choice but to descend to a lower level to avoid freezing everyone on board. Not only did these heater failures cause condensation to form inside the airframe and water droplets to fall like rain on the occupants, they also brought the penalty of flying within or below the clouds so that the ability to navigate by the stars was often lost. In any case, astro-navigation was more difficult in a Tudor than in the older machines. In place of the astrodome with its central hook from which the sextant could be suspended, an almost flat surface of glass was fitted into the cockpit roof. The replacement of the astrodome may have been due to the unfortunate experience of the navigator in a Constellation, who was sucked out from the flight deck to suffer a grisly fate when the astrodome cracked apart under the differential pressure. The lack of a hook meant that the navigator had to bear the full weight of the sextant for the two minutes during which he was also trying to keep the star in the middle of the sextant's bubble. This was not an easy task, even when flight conditions were smooth.

Although the Tudor cruised at a faster speed than the Lancastrian, its range was less. Given a situation of heater failure, low level cruising and an invisible night sky, navigation had to be by dead reckoning and a pious hope that the winds were not more adverse than those forecast. In the event, however, there were two occasions when, cruising in warm comfort at the upper operational level, the aircraft position "fix" plotted at regular intervals on the navigation chart revealed such adverse winds that a diversion was made to Gander. On a third occasion, a captain who had passed the point at which a diversion to Gander was still possible obtained a "fix" so far short of his expected position that he seriously doubted whether Bermuda could be reached before his fuel ran out. He alerted the island's rescue service to his predicament and was escorted towards the airport by aircraft carrying liferafts, landing safely.

To avoid a recurrence of such an incident, Bennett authorised captains to nominate Gander as a refuelling stop when planning the flight and to fly there either from Azores or even from Iceland. These measures did not enhance the appeal of the Tudor to the passengers, particularly in winter, and even less so when the cabin heater failed. However, the crisis point for Bennett and ultimately for BSAA came when the Tudor *Star Tiger* disappeared without sending any distress signal shortly before it was due into Bermuda.

Star Tiger left London Airport on a January morning in 1948, its ultimate destination being Havana. On the way to Lisbon the heater failed, and on the following sector to the Azores this happened again. The schedule called for the same crew to continue to Bermuda but having visited the weather office and estimated the flight plan time, the captain decided to delay his departure for 24 hours. These flights were normally undertaken at night to make use of star sightings. There was also a company Lancastrian at the Azores carrying freight that was to be transshipped to the Tudor for onward carriage after both aircraft had arrived in Bermuda. The captain of the Lancastrian also delayed his departure for 24 hours. The next day both captains studied the latest weather information and estimated the flying time to Bermuda to be an acceptable 12½ hours. For ease of handling at Bermuda, the Lancastrian took off first, followed an hour later by the Tudor. To avoid the stronger south-westerly winds at higher altitudes, the Lancastrian captain elected to fly at 2,000 feet. When the Tudor took off, its tanks were full to capacity, the captain knowingly overloading the aircraft by the small margin of 1,000 lbs. The radio officers on each machine maintained contact with one another, and when the navigator of the Lancastrian obtained his first astro "fix" he was able to warn his colleague that the wind strength was 55 knots and thus well above the 30 to 40 knots forecast. When contact was made with Bermuda the radio station also reported winds stronger than those notified to the crews at the planning stage. The Tudor had been in the air six hours before a star fix could be plotted, and this confirmed the stronger winds. It had then flown past the "point of no return", but both navigators were still expecting their flights to be completed within 13½ hours, one hour more than the flight plan.

The Lancastrian was already committed to a continuation to Bermuda when a star fix showed it to be 68 miles north of its intended track, and the course was altered into the teeth of the strong south-westerly wind. Soon afterwards the Tudor navigator confirmed that his aircraft was also well to the north of the track. He revised his estimated time of arrival and worked out that this would be about fifteen hours from the time of departure but with one hour's fuel remaining. Soon after the Lancastrian had changed from wireless telegraphy to radio telephony in preparation for the landing at Bermuda, the Tudor's radio officer obtained a Class I bearing of 072°. It was the last contact made, and twenty-five minutes later, after calls had gone unanswered, the alarm was raised. At dawn, 26 aircraft including the Lancastrian began a search, but no wreckage, not a patch of oil, no dinghy nor bodies were seen; *Star Tiger* had disappeared without any clue as to the nature of the disaster which had overtaken her.

In Britain there was a swift official reaction; the Air Registration Board advised Lord Nathan, the Minister for Civil Aviation, that it would be prudent to ground the airliner pending an investigation, and this was done. Bennett was scandalised, and without consulting the Chairman of BSAA or any of the members of the Board he gave an interview to the *Daily Express*. He maintained that as Chief Executive of the airline the decision to ground the Tudor was a matter for himself. In the event he had been unable to find the slightest grounds for any suspicion of faults in the aircraft. He was quoted as saying, "There are two outstanding forces at work in civil aviation today . . . those who are openly anti-British . . . and those who entered it either for selfish reasons or for other reasons—but are totally ignorant of aviation . . . interference with management has now reached such a degree that it has been increasingly difficult for an airline executive to be held responsible for the results he achieves."

This time it was the Board of BSAA that was affronted, and Bennett was asked either to retract his statement or to resign. He refused to do either, thereupon the Board dismissed him.   It was a bitter blow to Bennett, who had looked forward to the day when both the de Havilland Comet and the Saunders Roe Princess flying boat would be carrying the airline's passengers. Nor did Bennett go quietly. A by-election was pending at North Croydon, where the Liberal candidate stood down in his favour, and the press were happy to print his criticism of the government and government agencies. "I have been sacked for speaking my mind", he said. "The country needs national resurgence. If necessary I will lead it . . . The minister has made it clear that those in anything like a responsible position in nationalised industry are very much muzzled with regard to the details of management and to their political views. In other words I was not the 'Yes-man' who alone can fit into a socialist structure . . . Recent events have made it possible for me to turn to the attack and attack I will. I will fight to the utmost against socialist strangulation."

The grounding of the Tudor and Bennett's dismissal were discussed in the House of Commons. It was stated that since January, 1946, there had been six accidents due to errors of judgment; four of these were fatal. The Parliamentary Secretary to the Ministry of Civil Aviation declared that the high accident rate was not unrelated to the fact that operations were conducted "very near to the bone"; training and maintenance standards were not as high as they should have been. Incidents such as the landing of a Tudor at Bermuda with very little fuel did have a bearing on the loss of confidence of BSAA's Board in Bennett. Bennett had his defenders; the editor of *Flight* wrote, "The whole unfortunate affair really boils down to the fact that Don Bennett would have been the right man in the right job if the Corporation had not been a socialised concern. He is not universally popular. A man who drives himself and others as hard as he does could not be popular with everybody, but he is greatly respected and there are few enough like him in British civil aviation who have the courage to stand up for British aircraft, the knowledge to know what he wants and the ability to abide by his decision." Those closest to Bennett within BSAA, the captains and crews, were saddened by the manner of his departure. Although he drove them hard they had an immense regard for his ability and had shared his determination to make the airline an economic and commercial success. With hindsight it is clear that the enthusiasm of the crews could not combat the deficiencies of the aircraft and equipment being used nor the inadequacies of the means of navigation and the radio aids at airports. Nor did these men, many of them in their early twenties, have the all round ability and experience of Bennett. Faced with similar difficulties, BOAC had the advantage of a nucleus of very experienced airline captains able to inculcate a stronger sense of caution within the ranks of the newcomers, whose knowledge of aviation had been predominantly put to the test in wartime operations where courage and perseverance were more highly esteemed than a desire for self preservation. Former bomber pilots promoted to a command in the senior corporation were told by the captain in charge of training, "It is my job to turn you gallant young gentlemen into fussy old women." It would have been hard to find many of the latter category among the pilots of BSAA. A radio officer with years of experience at sea before he had joined the airline recalled his dismay when his captain warned the crew that he would make an emergency landing on a beach if the weather at both their destination and the alternative airport did not improve. "There are altogether too many bloody heroes in this outfit, if you ask me", was his comment at the time.

BOAC had already introduced check lists for its flight crews to use in preference to a dependence upon memory. Visibility and cloud base limits for each airport served by the airline were also published, along with a formula for computing an adequate fuel amount for the many stages of the company's route structure. Bennett rejected the advice of Captain Gordon Store, his operations manager, to adopt the same measures. It had always been his philosophy that the aircraft captain should never be obstructed from taking his own decisions as to when to fly or where to land.

When Bennett had applied to join Imperial Airways in 1935 he had been engaged by the Air Superintendent, Major Brackley. It was Air Commodore Brackley, joint vice chairman of BOAC with Whitney Straight, who was invited and who agreed to fill the vacancy for the post of chief executive of BSAA.

The Berlin Airlift   10

THE NORTH CROYDON by-election gave Bennett an opportunity to fulminate against the Labour government and what he saw as ministerial interference in matters which government departments were not competent to handle. When the votes were counted in March, 1948, the Conservative party held the seat with a clear majority over the Labour candidate, Harold Nicolson, with Bennett in third place.

He was not to be excluded from the aviation scene for long. He was certain that the disaster which had befallen *Star Tiger* was the work of a known saboteur. Intelligence sources had reported this man to have arrived in the Azores two days before the Tudor had taken off on its last flight; immediately afterwards the suspect had boarded a commercial aircraft bound for the United States. At the time, the British Government was trying to obtain an American loan and refused to respond to Bennett's urgings that the Federal Bureau of Investigation be asked to pursue this line of inquiry.

An opportunity to dispel doubts about the airworthiness of the Tudor came in an unexpected way. The Russian government imposed a road, rail and barge blockade on the sectors of Berlin occupied by British, American and French forces under the Four Power Agreement. The immediate cause of the blockade was the issue by the Western Allies of their own currency within West Berlin to put an end to the black market. The Russians had been about to impose their own currency throughout the whole city, and in reality the blockade was a Soviet device to test the will of the Western Allies to retain control of their own sectors. The city was situated in the very heart of the Russian dominated East German republic, and the only possible way for the Western Allies to maintain supplies of food and fuel to the beleaguered residents of West Berlin was by mounting an airlift around the clock. It was a decision taken without hesitation and was going to require the employment not only of all the military air transport the Western Allies could provide but suitable civil aircraft as well. In the same month that the Russians imposed the blockade, Bennett founded a new airline called Airflight. The Air Registration Board had decided that the Tudor could resume operations and Bennett bought two of them from the manufacturers, A. V. Roe. Within twenty-four hours of obtaining a permit to operate, he flew one of the aircraft to Wunstorf in Germany with ten tons of dehydrated potatoes.

Air Vice Marshal Bennett and Mrs Ly Bennett seen here before they join the first Tudor flight to east coast of South America, 1948. Capt. R. Alabaster

Airflight had its base at Langley and Bennett registered himself and his wife Ly as directors. As he was initially the only qualified Tudor captain, Ly was kept extremely busy looking after the office in England. The technical manager was Sarsby, the former group-captain who had been senior engineering officer in Pathfinder Force and had subsequently joined British South American Airways. Bennett had to find some pilots, radio officers and mechanics in a hurry in order to operate the two Tudors as intensively as he intended. This problem had to be resolved by most of the private companies as they joined in the airlift, eventually carrying forty per cent of the British load into Berlin. As the official report on the airlift subsequently put it: "the internal organisation of the companies did not keep pace with the increases in aircraft strength. Lack of experience in operating the number of machines taken on was aggravated by shortage of aircrew, maintenance personnel and spare parts. The aircrew position was particularly serious. In Airflight only Air Vice Marshal Bennett was authorised to fly at night on Tudors." The airlift provided a splendid opportunity for the private companies to earn substantial profits at a time when all scheduled services from the United Kingdom were allocated to the state airways corporations and when stringent currency restrictions imposed by the government had made it almost impossible for charter firms to offer holiday flights abroad.

Organising the allocation of flights along the air corridors into Berlin was made the responsibility of British European Airways. Initially this provoked strong opposition from private operators; they were reluctant to accept orders from a nationalised state corporation, the majority of whose staff were relatively inexperienced. As well as Bennett, there were representatives of charter companies who had a distinguished record of service in aviation. They included Air Commodore Critchley of Skyways, Sir Alan Cobham of Flight Refuelling and Wing Commander Aikman of Aquila Airways. There were some bad-tempered arguments before a better relationship was achieved.

After his arrival at Wunstorf, Bennett flew to Berlin each consecutive night, completing three round trips in the course of twelve hours. The second Tudor carried out flights in daylight under the command of Captain Utting. By October, the Tudors were converted to carry diesel oil in tanks fitted inside the fuselage. This was not only pumped on board far more swiftly than heavy goods could be loaded but was a more suitable cargo than sacks of coal, since the elevator controls of the aircraft ran under the floor of the fuselage and the accumulation of coal dust posed a worrying hazard. Even with almost ten tons of diesel oil in the fuselage tanks there was room for sacks of flour.

Airflights Tudor at Wunstorf.
Bennett family

As autumn arrived, the Western Allies could congratulate themselves that the loads being carried into Berlin had reached a peak of 5,000 tons each day. It was inevitable that periods of bad weather could be expected to interrupt the airlift of supplies flown into the city by day and by night. On one murky morning, Bennett was due to lead that day's flow of aircraft from Wunstorf with a departure time set for eight o'clock. Low cloud and poor visibility both locally and over Berlin made it doubtful whether the authorities would give the word to go; however, while Bennett was talking to the forecaster in the weather office his co-pilot was already seated in the Tudor and preparing the flight plan. This was Kenneth Hagyard, who had flown Lancasters in Bomber Command during the war, was engaged by BEA after his demobilisation and had then been among ninety pilots made redundant in an economy campaign. He had joined Airflight only a few weeks earlier. Also in the Tudor was the third member of the crew, a radio officer. Hagyard was still working at the navigator's table when Bennett appeared in the cockpit and clambered into his seat.

"We are going", he called out. "Start the engines at once." Hagyard moved from the navigator's seat across to the flight engineer's position, started the engines and then resumed work on the flight plan. But Bennett had a deadline to meet and urged haste. Hagyard again interrupted his work and from the engineer's position ran up each engine in turn and checked the magnetos. By this time Bennett had taxied out to the end of the runway; within seconds the aircraft would be cleared for take-off.

"We are off!" Bennett called and opened the throttles. The Tudor was already thundering down the runway when Hagyard reached the co-pilot's seat and strapped himself in. Visibility was only about 600 yards, and as take-off speed was approached the pilots could see beyond the runway's end the trucks and steam-rollers where the extension work was in progress. At a speed of 110 knots Bennett applied backward pressure on the control column to ease the aircraft off the runway. The control column did not budge; it remained rigid, held by one external elevator lock which no one had remembered to remove before the crew had boarded the Tudor. Bennett had to make an immediate decision—whether to slam the throttles closed and try to stop the aircraft as it raced on towards the mounds of earth, the vehicles and steamrollers, knowing that a collision would result in a mighty explosion as the tons of fuel on board ignited. Rejecting that action Bennett made an equally perilous choice—to rotate the small wheel that con-trolled the elevator trim tabs and by forcing the tail down, lift the aircraft nose sufficiently to cause the Tudor to climb. Almost any other pilot with the presence of mind to think of the trim wheel would not have realised, as Bennett did, that with the elevators immobile it was essential to rotate the wheel in the reverse sense. Gently his fingers inched the wheel forward, and as the nose rose the aircraft began to climb.

From the second pilot's seat, Hagyard watched in horror as the workmen jumped from vehicles or flung down their spades and flattened themselves on the ground to save their lives. Miraculously the Tudor cleared the obstacles and also the poles that supported the approach lights. The undercarriage and flaps remained extended but Bennett could not risk retracting them for fear of disturbing the delicate control he had so far achieved over the elevators and so putting the aircraft into a sudden dive or climb. He still had rudder control and the use of the ailerons, and by reducing engine power he levelled out below the over-cast at about 300 feet and began a gentle turn through north on to a heading parallel to the runway in preparation for an attempt to bring the Tudor back for a landing at Wunstorf. The control tower were informed of their predicament and Bennett's intention; all aircraft movements into and out of the airfield were cancelled and the emergency services were put on the alert. The team that manned the Ground Control Approach van, normally only available when the stream of aircraft was due back from Berlin, were summoned to give the Tudor all the help they could.

The airfield disappeared from sight as Bennett concentrated on maintaining a safe height and on the completion of the turn.

The surrounding countryside was flat and without natural obstructions but there were few landmarks to check their position. Hagyard had available a map of the local area, but with the visibility so poor it was of little use and at the end of his downwind leg Bennett carefully turned the Tudor on to the heading which he hoped would bring him back to the runway. The GCA crew were assembled but the aircraft was so low that it was not visible on their radar screen. When Bennett and Hagyard did see the airfield it was only half a mile away and the runway so far to their left that no time remained to line up for an approach. Two more complete circuits were flown and on each occasion the aircraft was so close when the runway was observed that it was impossible to make a safe correction of course in time to attempt a landing. Hagyard realised that the likelihood of a survivable landing was remote and he was very conscious of the vast quantity of diesel oil in the fuselage tanks which would break loose if the aircraft landed anywhere but on the runway. He suggested to Bennett that he remove the astrodome from the cockpit roof so that the space could provide an escape route. Bennett was anxious to avoid any action that would alter the trim of the aircraft. "Loosen the screws", he told Hagyard. "Leave the astrodome hanging on the last threads."

On the fourth approach, the GCA controller was able to afford more assistance and Bennett succeeded in lining up on the runway in sufficient time to attempt a landing. His task now was to achieve a safe loss of height on the final stage of the approach. He did not dare to make further adjustments to the trim tabs; everything would depend upon skilful use of the throttles. As he inched these back the airspeed reduced, but the aircraft nosed down and the speed increased again to 130 knots. Bennett opened all four throttles to arrest the dive, but as he again closed the throttles the dive was resumed. He gave the throttles a last burst and the speed rose to 150 knots. A huge crowd had assembled to watch the outcome of Bennett's handling of the Tudor, and the impression they formed during the final seconds was that the aircraft could not survive the impact, so steep was the angle of approach. They saw the wheels smack on to the runway, the tyres flatten to the rims, and they watched dumbfounded as the Tudor raced on down the runway apparently intact. The danger was not over, however, for until the tail-wheel was lowered towards the ground the brakes could not be applied or the aircraft would tip on to its nose. As the tail wheel sank, Bennett applied the brakes and stopped the Tudor before the end of the runway.

It was a very chastened crew that reflected upon their escape from a violent death. Bennett claimed that when he ran out from the control tower to the aircraft he had satisfied himself that the external locks on the port side of the Tudor had been removed; it was not his practice to use locks on the starboard side. Hagyard was acting as navigator and flight engineer as well as second pilot, but he had not reached the second pilot's seat until the aircraft was rolling down the runway. Every pilot is trained to check the free run of the controls before commencing a flight, and Bennett was certain that he had pushed the control column forward as he climbed into his seat. But he accepted that as captain of the aircraft the ultimate responsibility was his and he made no effort to place the blame on anybody else. On one thing everybody was agreed: only an airman with the exceptional ability of Bennett could have saved that Tudor, and there were few enough of those. That evening the same aircraft, its tyres undamaged from the hard landing, was flying once more to Berlin.

In December, 1948, Airflight's only captain other than Bennett was authorised to fly the Tudor at night. This pilot was Utting, but the first night on which he was in command he was walking out across the tarmac at Gatow to board the Tudor when he was knocked down and fatally injured by a truck. An investigation failed to identify either the driver or the vehicle and the suspicion arose that the occurrence was no accident but a deliberate attempt to kill Bennett, who on every previous night sortie to Berlin had been the captain of the Tudor. This tragedy obliged the latter to fly two or three sorties to Gatow airport every night for the following two months, a feat which was described in the official report on the airlift as "an epic of human endeavour which can have few parallels in the history of aviation."

To replace Utting, Hagyard was promoted to captain and soon afterwards was authorised to fly the Tudor at night. Airflight's two aircraft were carrying the largest loads of any machines being used on the airlift and for most of the time were flying more individual sorties than any of the others. In addition to the valuable revenue being earned there was now another reason for Bennett to prove that the Tudor was both airworthy and a commercial success. In January, 1949, on a scheduled flight for British South American Airways, *Star Ariel* left Bermuda en route to Nassau, reported that it had reached cruising level and then disappeared without trace in daylight and in perfect weather. The airline decided to withdraw the Tudors from passenger service, declaring that "the responsibility for continued operation was too great." The Ministry of Civil Aviation met and decided not to cancel the aircraft's Certificate of Airworthiness, effectively allowing their continued employment on the airlift. Bennett remained adamant that there was nothing in the construction of the Tudor which made it unsafe to fly.

In February, Airflight flew ninety-two sorties. In March, partly due to a better aircrew position but mainly owing to the adoption of a different maintenance system, 144 sorties were flown. The small workforce had to work harder than most of them had ever worked before. After twelve hours on duty each man had twelve hours off, for five consecutive weeks. Then five days' leave could be taken. The crews and ground mechanics received a salary, but no overtime payments were made and when the two Tudors needed servicing the pilots and radio officers were expected to give a hand. There was a profit sharing scheme: at the end of the financial year one third of the profits accrued to the Bennetts, one third was

Air Vice Marshal Bennett and his ground crew.
Captain K. Hagyard

ploughed back into the company and the small number of staff shared the remaining third. "It was very hard work," Hagyard recalls, "but whatever we did the Air Vice Marshal did more."

The crews were comfortably accommodated in what had been a Luftwaffe officers' mess at Wunstorf and were efficiently looked after by the German domestic staff who continued to work there. The intense pressure on the crews meant that they were often in a deep sleep when they were roused to prepare for the next series of flights. In one week in March the two Tudors had made fifty sorties to Berlin, a record not to be broken. On one occasion, the arrangements for their call broke down and Bennett, waking first and checking the time, personally woke his crew, thundering on their bedroom doors. If they had failed to be ready to start the aircraft engines at the pre-allotted time the Tudor would not be allowed to join the flow at all and valuable revenue would be lost. To save precious minutes they put their raincoats over their pyjamas and with their clothes rolled into a bundle rushed out to the waiting transport, eventually dressing themselves on the aeroplane.

In April, Hagyard resigned from Airflight. Bennett was very reluctant to let him go, but the young pilot was exhausted by the demands of the schedule he was expected to operate, combined with the exceptional hours of continuous work sometimes called for when it was necessary to assist in aircraft maintenance. In all the circumstances he did not trust his own ability to continue flying as safely as he should. He returned to BEA to complete his career and ended it as a Tristar captain by retirement age.

In May, Bennett withdrew the Tudors from the airlift because no further fuel was required in Berlin. They were flown back to Langley for conversion once again to freighters, and in their place a Lincoln was acquired and conducted sorties from Wunstorf until July. The Russians realised that the blockade had not only failed in its purpose but had provided a great propaganda victory for the Western Allies, who had been able to reassure both the citizens of Berlin and the people of the West German Republic that they would not be abandoned. The road and rail links were opened to traffic once more.

For Bennett, the airlift had not only made his airline a substantial profit, it had proved the worth of the Tudor. Airflight had made 977 return flights to Berlin, of which 250 had been flown by Bennett himself. When his former employer, British South American Airways, had withdrawn the Tudors from passenger service they had put them to work on the airlift. Soon after the airlift ended BSAA was absorbed into BOAC, but Bennett had his Tudors, his staff and a healthy bank balance. He was not going to give up now.

Charters, Cars and 11
Civil Actions

WHEREAS the Tudors had made a most valuable contribution
to the airlift and made good profits for Airflight, the aircraft
had still to obtain the approval of the Air Registration Board
before passengers could once more be carried. When his two
Tudors returned from Germany, Bennett and the aircraft manufacturers A. V. Roe went ahead with some modifications that the
ARB had recommended. Until a Certificate of Airworthiness for the
carriage of passenges was granted, the Tudors could be used only
to move cargo; in July, 1949, one of the aircraft brought from Paris
what was then the largest consignment ever carried by air into
England, nine tons of apricots. The small passenger door on an
aircraft which had not been designed to serve as a freighter meant
that it took two hours to unload the fruit.

By the end of August, Bennett's confidence in the Tudor was
rewarded when it was certified by the ARB to carry seventy-two
passengers. Shortly afterwards this figure was increased to seventy-
eight, at that time the largest seating capacity of any airliner in the
world. Charter operations carrying passengers could once more be
resumed, and to mark the occasion Bennett registered a new
company, Fairflight, and moved his flying base from Langley to
Blackbushe Airport, Hampshire. The new company's first passenger contract was successfully concluded when a Tudor was
employed to carry a number of apprentices from Karachi to
England on behalf of the government of Pakistan. It was a very
small company: two Tudors operated by a handful of pilots, radio
officers and flight engineers together with some mechanics.
Bennett established an excellent personal relationship with these
men, always explained to them how the company was faring
financially and kept them informed of future contracts.

Victor Bingham had served in the RAF from 1938 to 1947,
after which he continued to fly as a flight engineer with several
charter companies before joining Fairlight. Thereafter he spent
the remainder of his working life in civil aviation. "Bennett was the
best employer I ever had", he declared. "He never asked any of us
to do anything which he couldn't do himself. When he could spare
the time from his other commitments he would often join us in the
hangar and give a hand preparing an aircraft for service. Mrs
Bennett would arrive in the afternoon with tea and refreshments.

If the work continued into the evening the Air Vice Marshal would take us all off to a good local restaurant. We were told to order whatever we liked from the menu, no ceiling being placed on the cost." A teetotaller who did not smoke, Bennett was never known to swear either. His greatest rebuke to his staff was to address an offender as "you prune". Bingham remembers that during the school holidays the Bennetts' young son and daughter were sometimes brought to the hangar and found jobs to do.

When a charter involved a journey over long distances—and the Tudors flew to Johannesburg and Japan—Bennett's policy was to conduct the flight without a nightstop; the members of the crew took it in turn to sleep on a mattress, and as a qualified wireless operator Bennett could relieve the solitary radio officer. A flight engineer shared his workload with a ground engineer, who was taken along to help with the servicing at the airports. On arrival at their destination Bennett always took the crew to a first-class hotel, and after a good rest the return journey to Blackbushe was also normally made without a nightstop. Having once arranged a schedule, Bennett liked to keep to it; on one occasion he hustled his crew away from the breakfast table with the admonition "No time for cornflakes!" and this became a popular catch-phrase among the staff whenever a sense of urgency prevailed. On another occasion a ship's crew of Lascars were looking forward to the lunch they had been promised when the Tudor on which they had been travelling landed to refuel at Bahrein. On arrival, Bennett found that due to a communications failure no food had been prepared. The Lascars were exceedingly upset and vociferously proclaimed their unwillingness to continue their journey without the expected meal. They were not mollified by Bennett's assurance that when the aircraft reached Cyprus there would be a nightstop with plenty of time for food; when refuelling was completed and they were told to board the Tudor, they refused to budge from the airport lounge. Unmoved by this demonstration of defiance, Bennett walked out to the aircraft and started one of the engines. Thereupon the Lascars rushed out in a body to avoid being left behind.

During October and November, Fairflight's two Tudors made twenty-five round trips between Aden and Palestine carrying Jewish emigrants from the Yemen, usually the first time that such passengers had ever travelled by air. The bundles they carried on board often contained small portable stoves, and the flight crew had to keep a close watch to ensure that the emigrants did not attempt to light fires in the aircraft cabin in order to brew up a hot meal of their own choosing in preference to the fare offered. On one occasion, shortly after taking off from Aden, Bennett entered the passenger cabin to satisfy himself that all was well, and to his astonishment every one of the emigrants promptly went down on his knees. Such behaviour obviously called for an explanation and he sent for an interpreter. "It is the fulfilment of the scriptures", he was informed. "It is written that we Jews shall go to the promised land on the wings of an angel. You are that angel." "It was the first and last time that I have ever been called an angel", was Bennett's comment.

Fairflight might have suffered a considerable financial loss over one contract to fly pilgrims to Mecca if Bennett had not received a warning from his agent in time. A charter had been accepted for twenty flights from Istanbul. Payment was to be made in advance to a bank nominated by the company, but ten days before the date on which the first flight was due to take off no deposit had been received. Bennett flew out to Istanbul to investigate and met his agent there. Unknown to the businessmen who had settled the terms with the agent, the latter understood Turkish. It had become apparent to him that when the Tudor arrived in Istanbul to begin the movement of pilgrims, the charterers were going to insist upon all the flights being undertaken against payment into a local bank in Turkish currency. Such an arrangement would be upheld in a court of law in Turkey, but it would effectively deny Fairflight access to the money, which could not be converted into hard currency and transferred out of the country. "My advice to you", the agent warned Bennett, "is to move from your present hotel and leave the country as quickly as possible."

Fairflight had a busy programme of flights throughout the winter of 1949 and the early months of 1950. Never one to turn down a profitable contract, Bennett interrupted a holiday with his family in Switzerland to fly a Tudor to the Far East, a charter which was offered at very short notice. His crew recall that on their arrival back in England after a long flight, Bennett was not too weary to board his Proctor and take off to rejoin his family on the continent.

Then in March one of the Tudors met with disaster. It had been booked to carry a full load of Welsh rugby supporters home from a match between Wales and Ireland. They were to be flown from Dublin to Llandow, an airport fifteen miles from Cardiff which possessed a runway of no great length. Captain Parsons, the aircraft's pilot, had worked for Bennett on the airlift and had practised short landings, but he was worried about the operation into Llandow and had mentioned his misgivings to the captain of a Cambrian Airways aircraft with whom he had conversed in Dublin; there were not at that time any published regulations defining minimum landing distances. Observers at Llandow who were watching the Tudor during its final descent towards the runway reported that the nose rose sharply in the last stage of the approach as if there had been a sudden application of power. During the next few seconds the aircraft crashed. This tragedy caused the deaths of seventy-five passengers and a crew of five and set a melancholy new record for loss of life in an aircraft accident. It may be that to avoid overshooting the runway the Tudor was being flown at too low a speed and the pilot applied power too late, but Bennett believed that the pilot's seat might have slipped back on its runners, causing him involuntarily to pull back on the control column. The court of enquiry came to no conclusion as to the cause of the accident.

Fairflight continued operations with the one remaining Tudor, undertaking both passenger flights and freight charters. In June, Bennett registered another company, a travel agency which he called Fairtravel, whose offices were opened in Camberley and Slough. A twin engined Airspeed Consul was acquired for short range work from Blackbushe. In August, the Tudor set off for Karachi to fulfil a charter for fifteen flights between Pakistan and Jeddah, carrying a total of over a thousand passengers bound for Mecca, and to ensure that the operation ran smoothly, Bennett took some extra mechanics to Karachi. As always, he was often to be seen working alongside his men, dressed as they were in oilstained khaki shorts but easily identifiable by the Homburg hat he wore to protect his head from the powerful rays of the sun. While in Pakistan he placed an order for a Jaguar car to be sent to him in Karachi. It was a time when all British manufacturers were under pressure from the government to accord top priority to exports, and residents in the United Kingdom could only dream of acquiring a new car at some far distant date, years away in the future. Bennett had intended to take delivery of a large saloon that could be used to carry a crew and their baggage, but when the vehicle arrived in Karachi it turned out to be an XK 120 Jaguar sports car. After the last of the pilgrims had been brought back to Pakistan, Bennett shipped the car to England and entered it for the Royal Automobile Club Rally. To his delight he came fourth, and the experience so captivated him that he entered the Monte Carlo Rally. For four successive years he and his wife drove together, and in the fifth year Bennett's co-driver was his son.

An Air Ministry contract to fly stores to the British troops who had bene sent to defend South Korea was obtained as soon as the Karachi contract was completed. Bennett flew out in the Tudor and had to change one of the aircraft's engines at the United States Air Force base on Okinawa. The work had to be carried out in the open on a blustery day. An American sergeant, appraised of the pilot's identity, approached to take a closer look at an unfamiliar aircraft and its captain. "Never thought I would ever see a two-star general change an engine in a gale", he was heard to remark.

For the first seven months of 1951, the solitary Tudor was

engaged on long distance charter flights before returning to Berlin to fly freight services between that city and Hamburg. Bennett repurchased the Lincoln that he had operated on the airlift, and this was also used. Then, in November, he sold Fairflight to a subsidiary of Freddie Laker's company, Aviation Traders. It was the end of his long association with the Tudor. He believed that he had conclusively proved the aircraft to be both airworthy and a commercial success. Laker must have agreed with that estimation because he bought every remaining Tudor he could find and undertook a thorough conversion programme. Thereafter, the Tudor emerged as the Avro Supertrader and was operated on trooping services and the carriage of equipment for the British government to the Woomera rocket range in Australia.

In a memorable comment upon the result of the general election of 1945 which was called after the surrender of Germany, Winston Churchill concluded with the words " . . . all our enemies having surrendered unconditionally or being about to do so, I was immediately dismissed by the British electorate from all further conduct of their affairs." Bennett had also been wounded by his rejection at the hands of the voters in his constituency. He expressed his disgust in his own characteristic fashion. "I got kicked out on the service vote, which I thought pretty typical of this

The Bennetts driving their Fairthorpe car in the Monte Carlo rally, 1959. Bennett family

country. I had fought as hard a war as anybody but the Army was solidly against me." In 1948 Bennett had been an unsuccessful Liberal Candidate in a by-election that he fought soon after his dismissal from British South American Airways; but in 1950, notwithstanding the time-consuming responsibilities undertaken as director and chief pilot of Fairflight, he stood once again in the contest for Norwich North. The occasion was the general election, which was again won by Clement Attlee and the Labour party, although with a drastically reduced majority. Bennett suffered his third defeat at a time when the fortunes of the Liberal party had reached their nadir, their representation in the Commons declining to less than a dozen Members. It was the last occasion on which he offered himself as a candidate for parliament and at different times and in different ways he expressed his increasing disillusionment with the manner in which the House of Commons functions and the way the government conducts national affairs. In his own words: "I found that a member was impotent in all worth-while matters with practically no voting power and no speaking power. His sole purpose seemed to be that of a slightly exalted social welfare officer. The Whip system has completely strangled all democracy; the Party system has made a farce of our administrative arrangements and our voting system is outdated."

Throughout the war, Bennett had disagreed with Churchill's insistence that Britain was fighting to survive and to win without any war aims. He believed that what was needed was a geneal willingness to apply the same rules of law and order to nations as applied to ordinary citizens; to establish peace and then to keep it. He became Chairman of the United Nations Association of Great Britain in 1946, but here, too, he found that misgivings, doubts and distrust had taken the place of the determination and sacrifice to which he had become accustomed during the war. As he put it: "Of the fifty members of the Executive Committee of the UN Association, all of them were so expert that they knew that everything was impossible." Bennett found that the Charter of the United Nations contained virtually nothing to ensure that peace would be kept. First and foremost there was no armed police force, while the smallest nation had the same voting power as the greatest and the Security Council with its right of veto ensured that it could not function if a great power was involved in a dispute. Within a few years he resigned from the UN Committee.

However, he was never idle, never without some project of his own. A few months after the sale of Fairflight he founded Fairthorpe Cars and went into the business of motor car manufacture from a small workshop in Chalfont St Peter. His factory produced the body and chassis, back axles were bought in, and the car was available with either a Triumph or a Climax engine. Most of the Fairthorpe cars were sold to motoring enthusiasts who assembled them themselves from kits. The company's very first sale was to a customer in Malta, and the Fairthorpe sports car with a Climax engine won races in the United States. Production reached 400 annually and Bennett owned the business until 1983.

He also tried to revive interest in the Saunders-Roe Princess flying boats, which, along with the Bristol Brabazon landplane, looked likely to end up in the breaker's yard. When Bennett had been chief executive of BSAA there had been plans to introduce this flying boat into passenger service. Powered by ten Bristol Proteus engines, it was designed to carry 180 passengers across the Atlantic at a speed of 300 miles per hour. The disappearance of a second Tudor in the western Atlantic had resulted in the demise of BSAA, whilst BOAC had decided to abandon flying boat operations. Neither did the senior corporation wish to resume the discontinued South American services. Bennett approached Harold Watkinson, Minister for Civil Aviation, and applied for the operating rights. He had been promised sufficient financial support from private bankers to launch his plans to operate the Princess flying boats, but in time-honoured fashion the months went by while he waited for a decision by the government. When approval was eventually received, the bankers had withdrawn their guarantees and invested their money elsewhere. This delay finally doomed the Princess, although the Proteus engine survived to power the Bristol Britannia.

The Fairthorpe car designed by Bennett and the Linnet monoplane.
Bennett family

Saunders Roe Princess
*at the Farnborough Air
Show.* RAF Museum

In 1958, Bennett published a book of reminiscences. In the introduction he declared that he had delayed the writing for ten years because, in his own words, "I had recollections of the flood of war memoirs which were published after the first world war and I was determined that I would write nothing which was not mellowed by time and adjusted to its right perspective." The book was enjoyed by a host of readers, many of them airmen and airwomen who had served under the author. But one man who read the book and observed the references to himself within its pages believed that he had been made an object of ridicule. This was Air Vice Marshal Staton, who, the author wrote, had to be reprimanded for failing to obey some of the regulations of the Atlantic Ferry and had then annoyed Bennett by reporting to his office in Montreal wearing shorts. Staton brought an action for libel against both the publishers and the author and denied that the actions attributed to him had ever taken place. The publishers promptly withdrew the book from circulation and deleted the offending passage from the subsequent editions; they apologised to the Air Vice Marshal and paid him an agreed sum of damages in an out of court settlement.

Bennett's response to the charge of libel was totally in contrast to that of his publisher. He rejected the accusation, refused to apologise and declared that he stood by every word he had written. It was early in 1960 before the case appeared before Mr Justice Slade in the Queen's Bench Division, and Bennett chose to conduct his own defence "in the interests of economy". In his evidence Staton denied that he had ever met Bennett in Montreal or worn shorts in the offices of the Ferry Organisation. He told the court that when the latter reported to him at Leeming to take command of the Whitley Squadron he did not recognise him as anyone whom he had ever met before. He attributed the inclusion in the book of the story about the shorts to malice, because when Bennett had served under his command he had on two separate occasions found it necessary to take disciplinary action against him. Staton called his wife as a witness and almost twenty years after the event she was able to recall that she had not packed her husband's shorts when he was about to depart for Montreal. Air Marshal Sir Roderic Carr appeared as a character witness for Bennett, who had an opportunity to tell the court that as the pilot of *Mercury*, holder of the world's long distance seaplane record and founder of the Atlantic Ferry Organisation, he was quite well-known before he reported to Staton on his arrival at Leeming.

When all the evidence had been heard the judge remarked that never since he had first sat on the bench had he been so thankful to pass the responsibility to a jury to decide a case. When the jury returned from their deliberations, their verdict was that the words complained of by Air Vice Marshal Staton were not defamatory; Bennett had won and Staton had to pay the legal costs of the action.

A few months later, Bennett stood again in court as a defendant and once more conducted his own case. Eleven years earlier he had sold a ninety per cent interest in Airflight to another company, which was now charging him with fraudulent misrepresentation and breach of warranty. As the case progressed, the judge's interjections may have indicated to the plaintiffs that he felt little admiration for a business arrangement the principal intention of which was to avoid a very considerable liability to taxation. At any rate the company withdrew their allegations and abandoned the prosecution.

At about this time, Bennett bought Blackbushe Airport, "to save it from extinction". It had a good weather record and had been used by some airline operators as a base; it had also served as a useful alternative to London Airport in conditions of bad weather. However, he had not been able to purchase the entire area of the airport because part of it was owned by Yately Parish Council, who would not sell. He went to court to try to reverse this decision but without success, Lord Denning finding in favour of Yately. The runway length remaining in Bennett's possession was only sufficient to allow the airport to be used by light aircraft or at any rate those able to take off and land within the restricted distance available. Two flying clubs made use of Blackbushe, and Bennett remained the owner for sixteen years, employing the airport manager and local air traffic controllers.

During this period Bennett attempted to market a light aircraft which he dubbed the Fairtravel Linnet and which had been designed by a Frenchman called Piel. It had an elliptical wing and was about two thirds the size of a Spitfire; it carried two persons at a top speed of 120 miles per hour and the fuel consumption made it very economical. Bennett foresaw a future for the Linnet as a training aircraft, but although seven were built, it was not possible to find a backer to finance further production. The British government had already invested six million pounds in Peter Masefield's Beagle aircraft and naturally did not want to assist a direct competitor.

By 1970, Bennett had grown increasingly disillusioned with the Liberal party, particularly over its support for British entry into the European Economic Community. Since the days of Cobden and Bright the Liberals had supported the principles of Free Trade and subsequently the encouragement of trade within the Commonwealth of Nations, as the British Empire came to be called. But membership of the EEC meant an inevitable weakening of links which had joined together the dominions and colonies with Britain in peace and war. Nor did Bennett retain any confidence that the Liberal party leadership would maintain a realistic defence policy, claiming, "We will not be able to put up even a moderate defence in our own interests unless we remain staunchly and independently strong. I am the first to want a truly *United* Nations functioning in this world. I am sure however that with its present ineffective organisation the UN can do nothing for us. We can therefore only prevent war against ourselves by being sufficiently strong to deter it. We have the spirit and the courage but have we the political leaders and the men of wisdom and knowledge to find the path?" The quality of leadership of the two major parties which had alternated in government offered him no such assurance. Recalling the standing of the country in 1945, Bennett wrote, "In twenty-five years this greatness has been destroyed and Britain stands held by many abroad and unhappily by many at home as a third-rate power. This is not because we have lost any wars, nor because of our incompetence in any modern field of human activity—it has been caused by our political leaders and those who have supported them." The embrace of bureaucracy is probably as stifling in both the Eastern and Western camps, but in Bennett's words, "as the victory receded into the past I began to appreciate that in England the only thing which we had achieved was the right to be lazy, the right to preserve and protect every little dictatorship which set itself up and to conserve and cultivate every bureaucratic encumbrance that was possible . . . I watched the housing programme of Hamburg, one single city of Germany, exceed all the houses built in England in a period of twelve months."

The "closed shop" and the strike weapon earned his outright condemnation. He wrote: "On the home front . . . we find that freedom and justice are dead in many walks of life. For example a man cannot work at his trade unless he agrees to accept the private tyranny of some trade union. Similarly, trade associations fine both their members and people who are not members, and the so-called courts of justice of England uphold such fines as legal . . . we all complain if an IRA bomb does a few thousand pounds worth of damage in order to further the cause of the Irish rebels. We do not however apparently object to the odd few million pounds worth of industrial sabotage caused by unions in a matter of a few days." Bennett's proposed solution was a national wage policy to relate the wages earned with the value of the product or service produced by the individual. This and his criticisms about the electoral system and the present manner of government were expressed in papers that he published, including *Let us try Democracy*.

It has, of course, throughout the ages been the practice of the older generation to deplore the failings which seem so evident to them in their successors. Nor is it unusual for the young and the not-so-young to regard with cynicism those of their elders who choose to attend service reunions and to remember their fallen comrades. Forty-five years, during which this country had not been involved in a major war, have passed since Air Vice Marshal Bennett hung up his uniform and turned his attention to other fields of endeavour.

It has sometimes been said that people can be categorised into givers and takers. A great many individuals are proud to be of service to the community in any way they can; there are others who are only too happy to accept as many benefits as possible without any commensurate contribution whatever on their own part. There can be very little doubt into which of these two categories future generations will place Don Bennett. Few can have worked so hard to achieve their aims. There were successes and failures; he criticised others and was criticised in return. He continued to concern himself with the future well-being of this country by expressing his views forcibly, and there was no shortage of voices in rebuttal. But when Britain needed real leadership in the years of her greatest peril there can be no argument but that in his own sphere he supplied it in full measure. He was a leader who led from the front.

He died on 14th September, 1986, aged 76 to the day. A few weeks later the Royal Air Force church of St Clement Danes was packed to capacity for a service of thanksgiving and remembrance. Gathered together in one part of the church were former Pathfinders, and among these were pilots who had followed Bennett into British South American Airways after the war. The current Chief of Air Staff and a number of senior RAF officers were present, but these were men who had been too young to have fought during the war years. One who had done so was the retired Air Marshal Sir Ivor Broom, who gave the address. He had first met Bennett when at the age of 22 and holding the rank of flying officer he was accepted into the newly formed Pathfinder Force. He had already completed one tour of bomber operations and continued to command one of Bennett's squadrons. Of his former chief he said, "He was a real patriot who rigorously pursued what he considered was good for the country, sometimes to his own personal disadvantage."

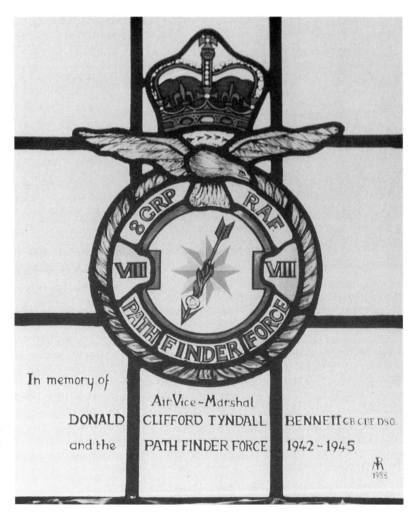

In memory of
Air Vice-Marshal
DONALD CLIFFORD TYNDALL BENNETT CB CBE DSO.
and the PATH FINDER FORCE 1942~1945

The window in Guildford Cathedral commemorating Air Vice Marshal Bennett and the Pathfinders Force.
Mr John Hunter

146

APPENDIX

Luftwaffe Intelligence Evaluation of Pathfinder Force Operations

No: 61008 Secret Ic/Foreign Air Forces West.
A/Evaluation West

GREAT BRITAIN

British Pathfinder Operations as at March 1944

Issued by

Luftwaffenführungsstab Ic/Fremde Luftwaffen West

———————————

BRITISH PATHFINDER OPERATIONS

CONTENTS

Preface

PREFACE

The success of a large-scale night raid by the R.A.F. is in increasing measure dependent on the conscientious flying of the Pathfinder crews. The frictionless functioning of the attack is only possible when the turning points on the inward and outward courses, as well as the target itself, are properly marked.

Lately, these attacks have been compressed into about four minutes for each wave averaging 120–150 aircraft.

Dense and high reaching clouds, which hide the sky markers over the target, and exceptionally strong winds which blow the markers away quickly, represent an unpredictable barrier to Pathfinder operations and can often appreciably decrease the efficiency of an attack.

Another reason for the failure of a raid may lie in the partial failure of the first Pathfinders, the "Initial Markers", to arrive, since experience has shown that succeeding Pathfinders, in spite of being equipped with H2S and blind marking equipment, have allowed themselves to be influenced, to a certain extent by the Initial Markers.

A. DEVELOPMENT

1. The concentrated large-scale RAF raid on Cologne on 30/31st May 1942, during a full-moon night and with an alleged strength of more than 900 aircraft, was the first attempt to imitate the "Focal Point" raids initiated by the German Air Force during this strategic air war against the British Isles during the years 1940 and 1941.

The lessons taught by this first large-scale raid, the increasingly high losses and the fact that the Hybola (Gee) navigation system could only be used in certain conditions, forced the A.O.C-in-C of Bomber Command to develop new systems of attack.

Using the German system of "Illuminators" and "Fire Raisers" as a model, the use of Pathfinders was developed towards the middle of August 1942, in order to bring on to the target all the aircraft, some with inexperienced, others with only medium-trained crews, and to allow of the dropping of the bombs without loss of time.

2. Air Vice Marshal BENNETT, at present still in command of these special units, was appointed Chief of the Pathfinder formations.

This 35 year old Australian—known as one of the most resourceful officers of the R.A.F.—had distinguished himself as long ago as 1938 by a record long-range flight to South Africa in a four-engined seaplane which was launched in the air from a Sunderland flying boat (composite aircraft). In 1940, BENNETT established the Transatlantic Ferry Command with aircraft of the "Hudson" type. As an example of his personal operational capabilities, an attack may be cited which he made on the German Fleet base at Trondheim.

BENNETT's appointment as "Commander of the Pathfinder Formations" is also based on the fact that he has written two standard books on astro-navigation.

3. The use of Pathfinders in the first large-scale raids was comparatively primitive. Several particularly experienced crews were sent out first as "Fire Raisers" ahead of the Main Bomber Force, and, in order to facilitate and ensure the location of the target, moonlight nights were especially favoured.

Shortly after the formation of these Pathfinder groups, however, the principle of raids during moonlit nights was dropped and raids in dark cloudless periods began to take place.

BENNETT strove to render the raids independent of the weather and at the same time to make it easier for the less experienced crews to locate the target.

4. At first there were only four bomber squadrons, equipped with "Stirlings", "Halifaxes", "Lancasters" and "Wellingtons", and in January 1943 these units were organised into 8 Bomber Group, the Pathfinder Group.

The grouping of the Pathfinders into a Bomber Group of their own made it possible to standardise the equipment and the training, to put new ideas into operation and immediately to evaluate all experiences.

During the course of 1943, the number of Pathfinder squadrons was increased to meet the increased demands and among others, several "Mosquito" Squadrons were detailed to the Pathfinder Group.

B. ORGANISATION AND EQUIPMENT
I. Organisation and aircraft types

1. 8th Bomber Group at present consists of:-

  Five "Lancaster" Squadrons.

  One "Halifax" Squadron.

  Four "Mosquito" Squadrons (including two special bomber squadrons with "Bumerang' (Oboe) equipment).

  One "Mosquito" Met. Flight.

  For further information concerning the organisation of these units see "Blue Book Series" Book I: "The British Heavy Bomber Squadrons".

2. In addition to the normal navigational aids (see also "Blue Book Series" Book 7: "British Navigation Systems") the aircraft carry the following special equipment:

  a) Four-engined aircraft ("Lancaster" and "Halifax"): Rotterdam (H2S) for location of target and bombing without ground visibility.
  Hyperbola navigation instrument (Gee).
  Identification Friend-Foe (F.F.).
  Acoustic night fighter warning instrument "Monica".
  VISUAL night-fighter warning instrument (cathode ray oscilloscope) "Fish Pond".
  Provision for bomb release in the cabin as well as in the navigation room.

  b) Twin engined aircraft (Mosquitoes).
  Hyperbola navigation instrument (Gee).
  Special equipment according to mission, for example "Bumerang" (Oboe).
  The existence of Mosquitoes equipped with H2S has not as yet been definitely established. According to latest information available, this special equipment does not yet seem to have been installed in the "Mosquito".

II. Personnel

1. The crews are no longer composed mainly of volunteers as was formerly the case. Owing to the great demand and the heavy losses, crews are either posted to Pathfinder units immediately after completing their training, or are transferred from ordinary bomber squadrons. As in the past, however, special promotion and the Golden Eagle badge are big inducements to the crews.

At first Pathfinder crews had to commit themselves to 60 operational flights, but because, due to this high number there were not sufficient volunteers, the figure was decreased to 45.

After transfer to a Pathfinder Squadron, a certain probationary period is undergone. The crews are not appointed Pathfinders and awarded the Golden Eagle until they have proved themselves capable of fulfilling the equipments by flying several operations (about fourteen) over Germany. Before the award of the Golden Eagle each member of a crew has to pass a special examination to show that he is fully capable of performing two functions on board, for example gunner and mechanic, or mechanic and bomb-aimer, etc.

2. There is a special Pathfinder school (N.T.U. Upwood Special School). All new crews, however are sent on a special navigational course lasting 8–14 days at a Navigation Training Unit, where particularly experienced instructors, who have already completed their pathfinder tours, train the crews in the operation of the special equipment and put the final polish on their already good navigational training.

New Pathfinder crews fly training flights over Great Britain. These are usually made South-West from the Cambridge area, course then being set for the Isle of Man. On the return flight a large city, such as Birmingham or Manchester is approached, dummy bombing using H2S is carried out, and target photographs are brought back to the home base. Flights of this kind are flown to a strict time schedule, just as in the case of a large-scale raid on Germany or the Occupied Western Territories and are taken into consideration in the assessment of the crews as Pathfinders. If on several occasions, the schedule is not adhered to the crew is transferred to an ordinary bomber squadron.

C. PATHFINDER OPERATIONS

I. General

The operational tactics of the Pathfinders have been under constant development ever since the earliest days, and even now cannot be considered as firmly established or completed. New methods of target location and marking, as well as extensive deceptive and diversionary measures against the German defences are evident in almost every operation.

Whereas the attacks of the British heavy bombers during the years lasted over an hour, the duration of the attack has been progressively shortened so that today, a raid of 800–900 aircraft is compressed into 20 minutes at the most. (According to captured enemy information, the plan for the raid on Berlin on February 15/16th 1944 called for 900 aircraft in five waves of four minutes each.)

In spite of the increased danger of collision or of dropping bombs on other aircraft which must be taken into account, the aim has been achieved of allowing the German defences, the Commands as well as the defence weapons themselves, only a fraction of the time available to them during the raids in the past. (See Appendices I and II for schematic diagrams of typical British night raids).

The realisation of these aims was made possible by the conscientious work of the Pathfinder group and by the high training standard (especially regarding navigation) of the crews.

The markers over the approach and withdrawal courses serve as navigational aids for all aircraft and above all they help them to keep to the exact schedule of times and positions along the briefed course. Over the target, the markers of the Pathfinders enable all aircraft to bomb accurately without loss of time.

II. Markers

Up to date, the following markers have been identified:-

i) *Target Markers*

a) *Ground Markers*, also called cascade bombs, are red, green and yellow. Weather conditions govern the setting of the barometric fuse, whereby the ground marker container is detonated at a height varying from 800 to 5,000 metres, thereby releasing 60 flares which fall burning and burn out on the ground.

Ground markers are mainly dropped in the target area, but they are also sometimes used as route markers. Ground markers are also dropped in 10/10th clouds in order to illuminate the cloud base from below. When the clouds are thin, the crew can see the glare without difficulty. The average duration of burning a ground marker is 3–4 minutes.

b) *Sky Markers* are parachute flares, of which several are usually placed simultaneously. As a rule the flares used are red ones from which at regular intervals quick burning green flares ("dripping green stars") drop out. Besides these, green Sky Markers with red stars and although comparatively seldom, green Sky Markers with yellow stars are also used.

The bomb aimers are for the most part briefed to drop their bombs into the middle of a group of sky markers. This corrects the opinion held until now that two sky markers are set, one to indicate the point of bomb release and the other to indicate the target.

c) *White and Yellowish Flares* are used chiefly to illuminate the target. They are also sometimes used as dummy markers.

During raids in the autumn of 1943, the enemy attempted to mark a target approach corridor by setting numerous flares. It may be assumed that he dropped this system because of the heavy losses inflicted by German single-engined night fighters in the target area.

ii) *Route Markers*

a) *As Track Markers* or Indicators, Sky Markers are used in 10/10ths cloud.

b) *Ground Markers* (Spotfires) are red, green or yellow; red and yellow are mainly used.

A ground marker does not split up into different traces, but burns with a single bright light for three to eight minutes.

iii) *New kinds of Markers, as yet not clearly identified*
The enemy has often tried to introduce new kinds of markers with varying lighting effects.

a) Among others, a quick falling flare bomb was observed lately. After it hit the ground a 90-metre high column of sparkle was observed, which slowly descended in many colours. Confirmation however, is not yet available.

b) To designate the beginning and the end of the attack, a large reddish-yellow "Fireball" has often been observed. Red flares fall from the Fireball and at low heights these again split up into green stars. The light intensity of these bombs is unusually high.

c) The so-called red "Multi-Flashes" are apparently used as Route Markers. They have been observed sparkling to the ground at intervals of 2–3 seconds.

d) The enemy seem to have stopped using enormous 1,800 kg size flare bombs. The reason for this could not be determined.

III. Execution of Pathfinder Operations

i) *Dividing of the Pathfinder crews*

a) At present, Pathfinder crews are divided into the following categories:-

Blind Markers
Blind Backers-up
Visual Backers-up
Visual Markers
Supporters. Pathfinder Main Force

About 15% of the bombers used for a large-scale operation are Pathfinders. For example, out of a total strength of 900 aircraft, 120 would be Pathfinder.

20 to 25 would be Blind Markers
30 to 45 would be Blind and Visual Backers-up
60 to 70 would be Pathfinder Main Force

b) *Blind Markers* It is the duty of the Blind Markers to locate the target using H2S and to set Ground or Sky Markers, or both according to weather conditions, at zero hour minus 2 to 5 minutes.

The Blind Marker crews alone are responsible for the success or the failure of the raid. They are more strictly bound to the time schedule than all the other aircraft taking part in the raid. They are not allowed to drop their markers if the schedule is deviated from by more than one or two minutes, or if the instruments fail, or fail to indicate accurately. In such cases the Blind Marker aircraft automatically becomes part of the Pathfinder Main Force and must drop its H.E. bomb load exactly at zero hour.

With smaller targets, it is the duty of the Blind Markers to set flares over the target area, in order to illuminate it.

Another duty of good Blind Marker crews during the initial stages of the attack is not only to set new markers, but also to re-centre the attack. Experience has shown that the first aircraft of the Main Force drop their bombs near the Markers but that succeeding aircraft tend to drop them short of the target area during the progress of the attack. It is the duty of the Blind Markers detailed for this purpose to bring the bombing back to the original target by re-setting the Markers past the first aiming point in the direction of the withdrawal.

For several months past, the Blind Markers have had a further duty. In several operations it was repeatedly shown that errors in the navigation of the Main Force occurred owing to inaccurate wind forecasts. Experienced Pathfinders were therefore instructed to transmit their established wind calculations to England by W/T. Each group picks up these reports and transmits them every half hour to the airborne bombers.

c) *Blind Backers-up* The duties of the Blind Backer-up are similar to those of the Blind Markers, except that they fly in the bomber stream. Thus, they drop their Markers during the attack, also in accordance with a strict previously laid down time schedule. Blind Backers-up are used to set Ground Markers and, above all, Sky Markers, which are always renewed by means of the H2S and never visually.

d) *Visual Backers-up* In order to give new Pathfinder crews a chance to gain experience for future operations as Visual or Blind Markers, they are allowed to set new Markers visually; these, however, are always of a different colour. Theoretically, these Markers should be on or very near to the original Markers, but as in practice this is very seldom the case, the impression given is that of the target being framed by markers. The bomb-aimers of the succeeding bombers are therefore briefed to release their bombs in the centre of the markers dropped by the Backers-up.

e) *Visual Markers* An attack on a small or pin-point target (definite industrial installations, dockyards, etc.) necessitates still more accurate marking than is possible by the Blind Markers. The Visual Markers, therefore locate the target visually from medium heights, sometimes from as low as 1,500 metres, and then release their ground Markers on the centre of the target, in order to concentrate the attack of the high-flying bombers. The Visual Markers are aided by the illumination of the target are aided by several Blind Markers (Newhaven attack) [sic].

f) *Supporters.* New crews who come from training units or other squadrons and who are to be trained as Pathfinders fly their first operations in the Pathfinder Main Force. They carry only mines or H.E. bombs, arrive exactly at zero hour and try, at the first concentric bombing, to create the conditions necessary to allow the incendiary bombs of the succeeding waves to take full effect.

ii) *Route Markers*

Route markers are set by good Blind Marker crews and are renewed during the approach of the "Bomber Stream" by further good Blind Marker crews. Ground Markers (Spotfires) are sometimes set visually, and sometimes by instruments, but Sky Markers used as Track Markers or Indicators are set only by means of H2S.

The routes of approach and withdrawal are generally identified by three Markers set at especially prominent points or turning points. The colours of these markers for any single night raid are usually the same, either red, green, yellow or white. It has often been observed that the Route Markers do not always lie exactly on course. They are set somewhat to one side so that the approaching bombers are not unnecessarily exposed to the danger of German night-fighters.

iii) *Target Markers*
The Target Markers used will differ according to weather conditions. More Sky or Ground Markers are set, according to the visibility and cloud conditions prevailing.

Up to date, the following methods of attack and target marking have been recognised:
   a) The "Paramata" attack under a clear sky and with good visibility. Ground Markers are used only.
   b) The "Wanganui" attack with 8–10/10ths cloud cover. Sky Markers only.
   c) The "Musical Paramata" attack with 5–8/10ths cloud cover. Mainly Ground Markers, but some Sky Markers.
   d) The "Newhaven" attack, in which the target area is illuminated by means of parachute flares coupled with several Ground Markers.
   e) The "Musical Wanganui" attack with 8–10/10ths cloud cover. Mainly Sky Markers, but some Ground Markers. This system of target marking has been used to a great extent lately during bad weather operations.

iv *Dropping the Markers*
The setting of the Pathfinder Markers requires a great deal of experience. For this reason, training flights with Markers of all kinds are often carried out over Great Britain, serving for practical experiments with flares as well as for training purposes.

When the target area is already illuminated by previously dropped flares, the Ground Markers are released visually by means of the ordinary bomb-sight.

In cases where 10/10ths cloud or dark conditions are found over the target area, H2S is used for dropping all Markers.

A great deal of experience is required for the setting of Blind Markers. Close co-operation between the navigator and the H2S operator (see "Blue Book" Series Book 7: "British Navigations Systems for the difference between the two), who sit side by side in the navigation room, is the first essential for the precise setting of Markers by means of H2S. Above all, drift must be calculated before the Markers are set, so that the Main attacking force only has to navigate on the Markers themselves.

v) *Navigation*
The basis for all Pathfinder navigation is dead reckoning, and all other systems are only aids to check and supplement this. H2S equipment is valueless without dead reckoning because the ground is not shown on the cathode ray tube screen as it is on a map.

To facilitate the location of the target, an auxiliary target, which experience shows to give a clear picture on the cathode ray tube, is given during the briefing. This auxiliary target should be as close to the actual target as possible, in order to eliminate all sources of error. Cities, large lakes, or even the coastline features are used as auxiliary targets.

The course and the time of flight from the auxiliary target to the actual target are calculated in advance, taking the wind into consideration. The H2S operator then knows that the main target will appear on the screen a given number of seconds after the auxiliary target has been identified.

IV "Mosquito" Pathfinder Operations

The "Mosquito" aircraft have special duties as Pathfinders, concerning which the following information is available:

i) *Setting ordinary Markers* 15 to 20 minutes before the beginning of the actual attack, in conjunction with other "Lancaster" Pathfinders, over an auxiliary target.

ii) *Setting dummy Markers*, along the coast and at other places to indicate a false course and a false target.

iii) *Dropping so-called "Fighter Flares"*, which are imitations of the white and yellow flares dropped by German Flare-carrying aircraft, to attract and divert German night-fighters.

These dummy Markers are often three to five minutes flight from the target, or are sometimes placed at points off the approach and withdrawal courses, although always in some sort of relationship to these.

iv) *Dropping "Window" from great heights* This is so timed, after taking wind conditions into consideration, that a cloud of Window will be over the target when the first four-engined Pathfinders get there. This is made necessary by the fact that the target must be approached in straight and level flight, without evasive action, in order to get a good H2S picture. It is supposed to eliminate to a great extent aimed fire by the Flak.

v) *Release of single H.E. bombs* 20 to 30 minutes after the main attack and observation of the results of the main attack.

vi) *Identification of pin-point targets* for succeeding "Mosquito" waves by setting Ground Markers with the aid of "Bumerang" (Oboe). The succeeding Mosquitoes then drop their bombs visually on the marked target.

D. CONCLUSIONS

1. Strong criticism from amongst their own units was at first levelled against the British Pathfinder operations, but they were able to prevail because of the successes achieved during the years 1943/44.

2. The original assumption that the majority of bomber crews would be less careful in their navigation once they became used to the help of the Pathfinders, and that therefore the total efficiency and success of raids would diminish, has hitherto not been confirmed.

The navigation, training and equipment of the ordinary British bomber crews has been improved.

3. The operational tactics of the Pathfinders cannot be considered as complete even today. There are in particular continual changes of all markers and marking systems.

4.   The trend of development will be towards making possible on one and the same night two or more large raids on the present scale, each with the usual Pathfinder accompaniment.

Distribution

Units of the R.d.L. and Ob.d.l.

Luftflotten down to operational Gruppen.

Flakabteilungen and Ln. Regiments.

Bibliography

BOOKS

Allen, H. R. *Legacy of Lord Trenchard.* Cassell, 1972.
Balfour, H. *Wings over Westminster.* Hutchinson, 1973.
Barker, R. *Great Mysteries of the Air.* Chatto and Windus, 1966.
Barker, R. *Survival in the Sky.* William Kimber, 1976.
Beaty, D. *The Water Jump.* Secker and Warburg, 1976.
Bennett, D. C. T. *Pathfinder.* Muller, 1958.
Bowyer, C. *Bomber Barons.* William Kimber, 1983.
Campbell, J. *Bombing of Nuremberg.* Allison and Busby, 1973.
Chandler, R. *Off the Beam.* Rendel, 1970.
Cochrane, A. *The Fighting Cochranes.* Quiller Press, 1983.
Collier, B. *Bridge across the Sky.* Macmillan, 1978.
Dean, M. *Royal Air Force and Two World Wars.* Cassell, 1979.
Harris, A. *Bomber Offensive.* Collins, 1947.
Hastings, M. *Bomber Command.* Michael Joseph, 1979.
Jackson, A. S. *Both Feet in the Air.* Terence Dalton, 1977.
Kidson. *Avro on the Airlift.* A. V. Roe Publicity, 1949.
Longmate N. *The Bombers.* Hutchinson, 1983.
McVicar, D. *Ferry Command.* Airlife, 1981.
Merton-Jones, A. *British Independent Airlines since 1946.* LAAS Int'nl &
    Merseyside Aviation, 1976.
Messenger. *Bomber Harris & the Strategic Bombing Campaign.* Arms and
    Armour Press, 1984.
Middlebrook, M. *The Nuremberg Raid.* Allen Lane, 1980.
Musgrove, G. *Pathfinder Force. History of 8 Group.* Macdonald and Jane's,
    1976.
Musgrove, G. *Operation Gomorrah.* Jane's, 1981.
Powell. *Ferryman.* Airlife, 1982.
Penrose, H. *Wings across the World.* Putnam, 1980.
Pudney, J. *The Seven Skies.* Putnam, 1959.
Reith, J. *Into the Wind.* Hodder & Stoughton, 1949.
Richards, D. *Portal of Hungerford.* Heinemann, 1977.
Saward, D. *Bomber Harris.* Cassell, 1984.
Saward, D. *Bernard Lovell.* Robert Hale, 1984.
Taylor, A. J. P. *Beaverbrook.* Hamish Hamilton, 1972.

GOVERNMENT PUBLICATIONS

E. Whitfield. *Report on the British Civil Airlift.* Air Ministry.
Air Ministry. *Merchant Airmen.* HMSO.
Ministry of Information. *Atlantic Bridge.* HMSO.

PERIODICALS   **OTHER SOURCES**

The Times   British South American Airways Archives
Flight
Aeroplane

Index

illustrations in **bold type**